LET THE
JOURNEY BEGIN

BY SHELDON D. NIX

LET THE JOURNEY BEGIN
by Sheldon D. Nix

Published by David C. Cook Publishing Co., Colorado
Springs, CO 80918, and
Renaissance Productions, Woodbury, NJ 08096.

Printed in the United States of America.

Edited by Eugene Seals
Cover and Interior Design by Cheryl Blum

ISBN 0-7814-5315-1

LET THE JOURNEY BEGIN

INTRODUCTION TO PROJECT MANHOOD

Project Manhood is a comprehensive mentoring program which has demonstrated its effectiveness in training boys to become men of God. It does not require a lot of money or advanced professional training. Ronald Evans, a committed layman at Antioch Baptist Church, has demonstrated that ordinary men can run most of this ministry.

The Project Manhood Series, of which this is the first manual, is comprehensive and will have the following components:

LET THE JOURNEY BEGIN
Boys 8- to 13-years of age are taught the values, habits, attitudes, and skills of "authentic" men (the focus of this manual).

PEER RESISTANCE AND DYSFUNCTIONAL BEHAVIOR PREVENTION
Boys are taught peer resistance and other skills to prevent dysfunctional behavior such as violence, drug addiction, and premarital sex.

COUNSELING AND CASE MANAGEMENT
Laymen provide boys with problem-solving counseling and ensure that their various needs get met through community resources.

CAREER DEVELOPMENT AND ENTREPRENEURIAL TRAINING
Boys are helped to career maturity and are taught to develop small businesses of their own.

BECOMING EFFECTIVE FATHERS AND MENTORS
Men are prepared to pour their lives into boys.

A STRATEGIC APPROACH

This manual is drawn from my experience as developer of Project Manhood and as a psychologist, social worker, and minister working with urban youth for two decades. Over the years, I have identified the key strategies that *work* in the difficult task of preparing boys for manhood. With the invaluable assistance of a number of committed men, I have been able to discover which approaches are most effective in helping boys to become men.

Project Manhood is not a perfect program. Not all the strategies advocated in this manual have been implemented in Project Manhood. But they each have been utilized successfully by somebody. They are tested strategies. You can implement them and count on them to make a difference in the lives of the boys and the men who work with them.

This first manual, *Let the Journey Begin,* is a practical guide to the most up-to-date strategies for working with youth. There are many books that warn us of the conspiracy against our boys and the difficulties they face in America. These books give us good analyses and good general principles. *Let the Journey Begin* goes the next step and provides concrete strategies for doing something about the situation. Further, it gives the reasons for those strategies so you will know why they work.

We suggest you prepare yourself to work with your boys by reading a number of the general books on the market. As you gain an appreciation for the big picture, read this manual and begin implementing the strategies step by step. Also, plan to attend conferences like E. K. Bailey Ministries' annual Developing and Empowering the African American Male conference in Dallas, Texas. Make a commitment to get the best training you can. Our boys deserve it. If you plan to work with them comprehensively, as this guide advocates, you will need the preparation.

TURNING A GENERATION OF BOYS INTO MEN

Helping boys become men takes time. Years of love and nurturing by caring adults go into such growth. The need is obvious. The rewards are enormous. Pro-

ject Manhood's four-stage process for training boys to be men includes:

- Manhood Development Training (Ages 8 - 13)
- Peer Leadership Development (Ages 14 - 15)
- College and Career Preparation (Ages 16 - 17)
- College and Career Mentoring (Ages 18 - 21)

This manual, *Let the Journey Begin,* focuses on the first stage. Boys 8 to 13 learn the values, attitudes, habits, and skills of an "authentic man." Knowing firmly who he is and where he is going, a boy becomes resistant to negative peer pressure and sets his feet on a solid path toward maturity and success.

Boys receive authentic manhood training. This is the core of the program at this stage. The boys learn what it really means to be men from a tested step-by-step curriculum which is constantly being reviewed and evaluated by the developers and by implementors in real life settings.

TARGETING KEY FACTORS THAT PLACE BOYS AT RISK

Project Manhood targets the central wounds of African American boys which predispose them toward dysfunctional behaviors. If we are to raise boys to become true men, we must understand that many have wounds, much anger, and

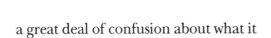

a great deal of confusion about what it means to be a man.

THEY ARE OFTEN WOUNDED

THE FATHER WOUND
For many, their dads are absent emotionally, physically, or both.

THE SOCIAL SERVICES WOUND
The faulty, overloaded social services system fails to help our boys succeed.

THE BODY WOUND
Boys often receive inadequate health care, nutrition, and disease prevention.

THE VOCATIONAL WOUND
Often our boys are disconnected from freedom of choice and progress in mainstream career opportunities.

THE EDUCATION WOUND
The education of our boys often leaves them terribly ill-prepared.

MANY ARE ANGRY

TOXIC SHAME
Deep shame is produced in many boys by their experiences, and they don't know how to deal with it.

DISPLACED RAGE
Many young urban males can't find the right target for the anger their shame creates.

REACTIONARY MASCULINITY
Such young boys, therefore, often put up a fragile wall of "macho" that hides their shame and pain. But it's just a reaction. Don't let it fool you.

SOME ARE CONFUSED

HISTORICAL CONFUSION
Many young boys don't know the greatness of their legacy as descendants of noble African men.

SPIRITUAL CONFUSION
Too many young boys are alienated from the Christian church.

COUNTERING RISK FACTORS

Project Manhood Series recognizes that a boy consists of not only a body, but also a mind and a spirit as well. Further, a growing boy is surrounded by a number of forces which influence his ability to make good choices in life. This program targets risk factors in six key areas of a boy's life as depicted in this diagram:

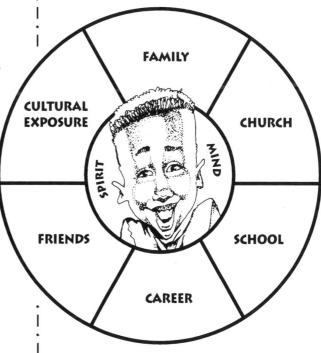

To address these risk factors, Project Manhood first looks at the big picture and develops an adequate response. The critical risk factors are described on the left in the following tables. Preventive and corrective goals are summarized on the right.

INDIVIDUAL FACTORS

RISK FACTORS
Risk factors are the inner dynamics and the external circumstances faced by boys that predispose them toward dysfunctional behavior.

GOALS
Project Manhood has developed specific goals to combat the risk factors in young men's lives. By focusing on these goals, the program is more likely to actually produce a change in boys' current and potential behavior.

MANHOOD TRAINING COMPONENT

RISK FACTORS	GOALS
Uncertainty about what an authentic man is and what it takes to become one	• Help boys develop a concept of what a mature male is. • Help boys identify the challenges and the choices they will face on their journey to manhood.
Dysfunctional attitudes and behavior patterns	• Help boys understand the areas of their character which need to be developed. • Increase boys' understanding of the consequences of drug use, violence, truancy, premarital sexual relations, etc. • Develop increased coping skills for handling conflict, peer pressure, etc.
Uncertain direction for life	• Help boys discover a sense of purpose. • Motivate boys to pursue their dreams, no matter what the obstacles. • Help boys identify the rewards of achieving their goals and dreams.

DYSFUNCTIONAL BEHAVIOR
PREVENTION & PEER RESISTANCE

RISK FACTORS	GOALS
Low self-esteem	• Help boys develop feelings of trust, safety, and assurance: SECURITY. • Help boys identify who they are: SENSE OF SELF. • Give boys a sense of belonging and love: AFFILIATION. • Help boys to recognize their successes and internalize feelings of accomplishment: COMPETENCE.
Susceptibility to peer influence	• Increase capacity to resist negative peer influences. • Enhance capacity to define socially acceptable and rewarding behaviors. • Improve ability to create alternative behaviors in response to threatening situations. • Refine the decision-making process to include newly adopted manhood values. • Increase openness to parents and willingness to allow parents to help monitor out-of-home behavior.
Favorable attitudes toward drug use, violence and pre-marital sex	• Increase boys' understanding of the consequences of drug use. • Develop an alternative peer reference group which disdains drug use and drug selling.

COUNSELING & CASE MANAGEMENT

RISK FACTORS	GOALS
Disconnection from community support systems	• Give an ongoing assessment of the needs of the boys and their families. • Determine which services will meet those needs. • Ensure that the boys and their families receive the services identified.
Unresolved emotional difficulties	• Provide age-appropriate, culturally competent counseling services to boys.

MENTORING COMPONENT

RISK FACTORS	GOALS
Disconnection from positive adult male role models	• Provide, as friends and advisors, men who are living positive lifestyles.

CAREER DEVELOPMENT & ENTREPRENEURIAL TRAINING

RISK FACTORS	GOALS
Lack of career information and direction	• Help boys develop a list of interests, skills, and values they enjoy using: SELF-ASSESSMENT. • Help boys find out what people with interests like theirs like to do: CAREER EXPLORATION. • Help boys select a career path (job or college) and help them get some experience in the field: CAREER DECISION/EXPERIENCE.
Lack of entrepreneurial attitudes, skills, knowledge, and opportunities (besides the drug trade)	• Help boys identify and develop the characteristics needed to become a self-starting, self-regulating, confident man. • Teach boys basic life skills: for example, money management principles. • Teach them how a business is selected, started, developed, and sustained. • Assist them in starting their own small businesses.

ACADEMIC ACHIEVEMENT COMPONENT

RISK FACTORS	GOALS
Academic failure	• Increase confidence about ability to learn. • Increase academic skills through tutoring. • Provide adult support for learning.

PARENT TRAINING &
PARENT SUPPORT GROUPS COMPONENT

RISK FACTORS	GOALS
Parental substance use and poor role modeling	• Decrease self-reported use of alcohol and drugs. • Decrease the incidence of parental dysfunctionality. • Increase parental psychosocial functioning. • Increase parents' willingness to seek help.
Poor or inadequate parent-youth communication patterns	• Increase understanding between parents and youth. • Enhance effectiveness in communicating about life issues.
Lack of parent-youth closeness	• Increase bonding between parents and male children. • Increase ability to solve problems on a collective basis. • Increase sense of family belonging. • Increase availability of information to solve problems.
Inconsistent or excessively severe negative discipline by parents	• Increase use of parenting solutions from a consistent value base. • Increase family interdependency and structure. • Increase use of positive discipline techniques.
Lack of parental monitoring and supervision of youths, especially for outside-the-home activities	• Increase knowledge base of parenting skills. • Increase use of interdependency with other adults as a means of monitoring youth. • Increase exposure to new experiences and social situations. • Increase use of community resources to solve problems.
Low expectations for boys' success and maturity	• Provide a forum for positive reinforcement for boys. • Help parents find a balance between parental control and boys' self-responsibility. • Increase parental expectations regarding drug use, violence, premarital sexuality, and other teenage dysfunctional behaviors.

COMMUNITY FACTORS

ALL COMPONENTS

RISK FACTORS	GOALS
Peer pressure to engage in dysfunctional behaviors	• Create an alternative male peer group with positive values. • Strengthen peer resistance skills as discussed above.
Lack of community rituals for helping boys negotiate their passage into manhood	• Increase messages from church and community teaching responsible manhood values and roles. • Increase formal and informal community rituals which give young males approval, validation, and structure for achieving maturity goals.
Insufficient awareness and involvement of community organizations in prevention of violence, substance abuse, teenage pregnancy, and academic failure	• Increase the number of churches capable of sustaining effective young male programs. • Empower lay persons within churches to operate efficient and effective high-risk male youth programs. • Enlist community businesses in efforts to assist young males.

OVERCOMING BARRIERS TO HEALTHY DEVELOPMENT

Jawanza Kunjufu calls it a "conspiracy." No doubt much of it is, whether overt as the term normally implies, or also widespread passive indifference from powerful people of many races, or both. Without a doubt, something or someone is destroying our boys in epidemic proportions. Anyone attempting to prepare boys for manhood needs to be clear that we are operating against tremendous obstacles. Getting boys to manhood successfully is one of the most difficult ministries we can attempt.

By "destruction" we mean an undermining of the healthy development of our boys in multiple areas of their lives:

MORAL
There is a crippling of the ability of boys to make good moral judgments and live moral, Christian lifestyles. What we have found is a deep confusion in many boys about moral standards. Most of them do not uphold antisocial values; they don't think murder, rape or theft is good. Rather, they don't know what is good.

PSYCHOLOGICAL
Our boys often suffer devastating psychological wounds:

• Developmental wounds. The healthy development of our boys is hindered. They sometimes do not master the developmental tasks of maturing. They remain immature in important areas of their lives.

• Emotional wounds. They sometimes develop emotional and psychological problems in their struggle to cope with life. These can include chronic depression, chronic anxiety, a deep sense of shame, low self-esteem, lack of clear identity, and rage.

• Cognitive deficits. Boys often fail to develop the mental skills needed to effectively negotiate life (including problem solving, planning, and critical thinking).

SOCIAL
Boys sometimes fail to develop socially:

• Social skills. Sometimes they don't develop certain skills needed to interact in mainstream society.

• Social support. Our boys often lack supportive, healthy relationships.

ACADEMIC
Some boys suffer terrible injustices in the schools.

SOCIETAL
African American boys get increasingly disconnected from mainstream opportunities.

SPIRITUAL

Studies indicate that boys must be reached by the age of 12 or they begin to fall away from the church and from any focus on spirituality. This leaves them with an inner sense of emptiness and purposelessness.

PHYSICAL

At best, our boys usually do not get involved in the health care system until there is a serious problem necessitating emergency room treatment. That is, they do not get primary care, and they often live unhealthy lives. At worst, they are seriously injured or even killed by violence and other societal ills.

WHY SOME BOYS DO NOT BECOME MEN

If you are serious about understanding what happens to our boys, there are some books which explain it in much more detail than we can hope to do in a manual. We especially recommend the works of Jawanza Kunjufu. Also, Daniel Black has done unique research on the evolution of the concept of manhood from West Africa through the Middle Passage on into the present day.

See the "Suggested Readings for Working with Males" bibliography (pages 101, 102) for additional resources. We have to be honest in saying that African Americans have not been able to publish a significant number of books on the subject. However, many of the books on the market apply to us because African American men share many, many issues with other men because we are very American. We suggest you also read Mychal Wynn's *Empowering African American Males to Succeed*. He doesn't focus heavily on analysis, but does suggest some concrete strategies and gives some useful exercises. He's the only author we know of besides ourselves who has published a non-theoretical work.

BASIC STRATEGIES FOR PROJECT MANHOOD

What do we mean by "manhood training"? In general, everything Project Manhood attempts to do accomplishes the goal of training boys to be men. What we mean specifically, however, is implementing the following strategies: Instill Motivation & Hope; Instill Purpose; Teach Goal Achievement Habits; Teach Life Skills; Create Opportunities to Achieve; and Celebrate Rites of Passage Rituals.

STRATEGY 1 – INSTILL MOTIVATION & HOPE

Since our boys grow up so hopeless, they need to be given a sense of hope that they can become men. It is one of the first things you must do with boys who at their young age are already discouraged, depressed, angry, and without direction.

Programs and ministries that start with the how-tos of living without first dealing with motivation and hope lose their boys. They come for a short while and then leave, because what they come for is a thrill, a high, excitement, pizazz. You can give them some of that. But if you don't hook them at the deepest level of their being, you will run out of tricks and entertainment, and they will leave. However, if you can motivate them to want to become men, they will give you the time it takes to teach them to be authentic men. How do you instill motivation and hope? Through utilizing relationships and teaching concepts.

RELATIONSHIPS

• **Love.** While it may sound corny, if you don't love the boys, don't bother working with them. Many have become so jaded, so wary of programs that come and go, that they have a hard, macho shell which they will be very reluctant to shed. They will test your commitment time and again. Only gradually will they become vulnerable. (Some boys are instantly vulnerable, not having been able to develop a hard shell. These boys have open wounds.)

• **Forgiveness.** You must create an atmosphere that welcomes the boys with wide open arms, an atmosphere in which they feel accepted and forgiven for wherever they have been. Do everything you can to get the whole group to adopt this attitude of acceptance.

• **A Safe, Interesting Community**. It is very important to form the boys into a cohesive group. Think through ahead of time how you want the group to operate, and focus on the fact that your goal in the first months of the group's formation is to become a community. If these are boys who already know each other, you will need to make this Project Manhood group (or whatever you call your group) something new, something special, something worth trying to get into.

CONCEPTS

• **What Authentic Manhood Is.** Boys are deeply confused about what it means to be a man. You have to teach them, and you have to do it in a way that makes them want to be such a man. We tackle this issue right away with the "Oath of Manhood." Based on the Beatitudes, the Oath teaches them what it really means to be a man.

• **What the Journey to Manhood Involves.** One of the things most frequently found out about our youth is not that they don't have significant goals for their lives. Most of them do. Rather, the youth have no idea what it takes to get from where they are to where they want to go. This manual, *Let the Journey Begin,* gives the boys a literal map (see p.16) of the journey to manhood based on the life of Joseph in the Old Testament.

We teach them about the obstacles they face as African American boys. We help them to understand the "call to manhood" that life gives to them. Then we conclude by helping them to understand some of the critical choices they must face along the way, such as whether to pursue excellence or accept mediocrity. If they make the right choices, they will move closer to manhood. If they choose the wider, easier path, they will end up like so many of their peers in the "Swamp of False Manhood."

Underneath all of our manhood concepts in Project Manhood, there is an underlying philosophy that becoming a man, especially becoming an African

American man, is a very difficult process. It requires courage and discipline because it involves suffering.

THE ROAD TO MANHOOD MAP

AUTHENTIC MANHOOD

PREGNANCY

LETTING GO OF THE PAST

SWAMP OF FALSE MANHOOD

BROKEN DREAMS

GOD'S TIME

DRUGS

POOR GRADES

SMART WAITING

LIFE'S WAITING ROOM

SHORT CUT

LOW SELF-ESTEEM

INTEGRITY VS. COMPROMISE

BITTERNESS

EXCELLENCE VS. MEDIOCRITY

THE CALL TO MANHOOD

BOYS IN THE 'HOOD

FAMILY STRUGGLES

YOUR CHARACTER

DESERT OF OPPRESSION

BOYHOOD

© 1992, 1996 Sheldon D. Nix

The "Authentic Manhood" audio tape offered by Renaissance Productions deals with this issue. What we want boys to understand is that they must develop the kind of perseverance and focus that their most admired athletes develop.

The Apostle Paul drew on the analogy of a runner straining toward the finish line, "Not that I have already attained, or am already perfected; but I press on, that I may lay hold of that for which Christ Jesus has also laid hold of me. Brethren, I do not count myself to have apprehended; but one thing I do, forgetting those things which are behind, and reaching forward to those things which are ahead, I press toward the goal for the prize of the upward call of God in Christ Jesus" (Philippians 3:12-14, NKJV).

STRATEGY 2 – INSTILL PURPOSE

One of the central needs of our boys is to develop a sense of their purpose in life. Because it is so vital, we address the issue of purpose several times in this manual. Who we are, says Myles Munroe, is determined by why we are. We can never fully understand ourselves without understanding God's purpose for our lives.

The problem is that our boys have forgotten how to dream effectively. Their dreams have been stamped out

---

ACHIEVING MANHOOD TAKES COURAGE AND DISCIPLINE

"Life is difficult. This is a great truth, one of the greatest truths. It is a great truth because once we truly . . . understand and accept it, then life is no longer difficult. Most do not fully see this truth. . . . Instead they moan more or less incessantly about the enormity of their problems, their burdens . . . as if life should be easy.

Life is a series of problems. Do we want to moan about them or solve them? Do we want to teach our children to solve them? Discipline is the basic set of tools we require to solve life's problems. . . . Problems call forth our courage and our wisdom. It is only because of problems that we grow mentally and spiritually. When we desire to encourage the growth of the human spirit, we challenge and encourage the human capacity to solve problems. It is through the pain of confronting and resolving problems that we learn."

M. Scott Peck, *The Road Less Traveled*

of them by the principalities and powers of the world which are seeking to break them. We want boys to understand their high calling as the pinnacle of God's creation and as a dignified people, as well as what has been done to them.

Reteaching our boys to dream is not easy. Retraining them to develop goals for their lives is difficult, but if you come at it from multiple angles, it can be done. The success of the "I Have a Dream" program in which wealthy philanthropists "adopt" a group of urban youth and promise them a college education if they graduate from high school, while providing them some current supports, is a witness to the power of offering our kids a real chance to dream.

> "The greatest tragedy in life is not death, but life without a reason. It is dangerous to be alive and not know why you were given life. The deepest craving of the human spirit is to find a sense of significance and relevance. . . . It directs his decisions, controls his behavior and dictates his responses to his environment."
>
> Myles Munroe, *In Pursuit of Purpose*

STRATEGY 3 – TEACH GOAL ACHIEVEMENT HABITS

Once a boy has some sense of his purpose, he needs to learn the skills for achieving that purpose. And those skills have to become habits. He has to learn to apply them in every area of his life.

STRATEGY 4 – TEACH LIFE SKILLS

So many of our boys don't know how to negotiate life in a practical way. They need to learn how to shop effectively, how to fill out forms, how to read maps and schedules, and how to do a thousand of the practical things that make life possible on a daily basis.

STRATEGY 5 – CREATE OPPORTUNITIES TO ACHIEVE

Boys need to be given standards of character and behavior that they are held to. Hence, in Project Manhood, we emphasize discipline and the teaching of values and personal responsibility. Boys need to be given opportunities to prove their manhood through the achievement of goals.

WHY OUR BOYS NEED TO PROVE THEIR MANHOOD

Research shows that "manhood" around the world is a status that needs to be earned. Anthropologist David Gilmore, in his classic *Man in the Making*, examined "primitive" and industrialized cultures around the world to determine what it takes to be a man. What he found was that in culture after culture "manhood" was something that had to be proven. He discovered that there were three major ways in which young men proved their manhood to their communities: the ability to procreate, the ability to protect, and the ability to provide.

Gilmore also noted that the more dangerous the world around them, the more the tribe or community needed the men to procreate, protect, and provide. Further, he found that the more dangerous the world, the more rigid these roles became, and the harsher the rites of passage in which boys proved their manhood.

Consider now the situation of many African American boys. They live in a dangerous world. Their biologically wired need (if that is what it is) to prove their manhood will, therefore, be even more intense than in communities with less danger. Their attempts to prove their manhood will be immature (because they don't have elders to guide them such as we try to provide in Project Manhood), but they are simply doing what most males do. They will procreate (or at least have sex) as much as possible. They will protect (one attraction of gangs is they can protect each other). But they may give up on providing or they may provide through the drug trade.

HARNESSING THE NEED TO PROVE ONE'S MANHOOD

Since proving one's manhood is a universal – or at least very widespread – drive in men, the strategy of Project Manhood is to harness that drive by channeling it in the right direction. If boys need to prove their manhood, make them prove it – and then tell them how to do it.

There is a lot of support for this concept. Studies of effective parenting show that parents who produce children with high self-esteem and high achievement set demanding standards for their kids, and then give lots of support to help them meet those standards. Similarly, our research at Michigan State University found that teachers who 1) set high standards, who then 2) teach the strategies for meeting those standards, and who 3) give lots of opportunities to practice the strategies produce students with high self-esteem and high academic achievement.

So in every area I look, setting high standards, teaching kids how to meet those standards, and then giving opportunities to put what they've learned into practice is one of the most important strategies for producing high-performing kids. In Project Manhood, we set high standards by giving boys a vision of what it really means to be a man and expecting them to behave accordingly. We then give them lots of training – Manhood Training, Prevention Training, Entrepreneurial Training, etc. Finally, we give them opportunities to demonstrate the manhood values, attitudes, habits, and skills we have taught them. How is this done?

1. MAKE FIELD TRIPS AND SPECIAL OUTINGS SOMETHING BOYS HAVE TO EARN.
There needs to be lots of special activities for the boys so that the program isn't just serious training, counseling, and business development, but also fun. Moreover, field trips expose our boys to the wider world. But make them earn the right to go.

2. DEVELOP "ACHIEVEMENT LEVELS" FOR THE BOYS TO REACH.
By constructing "Manhood Achievement Levels," you give them goals to strive for much as in the martial arts (with belt colors) and the Boy Scouts (with their various levels). Decide what they should be

striving for – what behaviors you want to see, what milestones they are to reach, what they are to learn – in order to reach the next level. The best way to do this is to think about what you will teach them and when you will teach it to them. Then take your teaching/training goals and turn them into achievement goals.

For example, you may decide that the concept of delayed gratification is a key goal for Level 1. You will then ask the boys to demonstrate that they have the ability to wait their turn, get their work done before they play, try to get the answer first on their own before asking the teacher/trainer, etc. – all behaviors which demonstrate a capacity to not take the easy way out but to wait and get it right. Make sure that all boys are clear on what each level requires. Use the worksheets on pages 20–22 to think through at least three levels for the boys to reach. Make reaching these levels something to celebrate, and give them tangible signs that they have reached these levels (for example, kente scarves, jackets, etc.).

These are your major milestones. You should also think through a system of rewards for mini-milestones. For example, you can set up a point system so that boys can earn points in order to go on field trips, get extra money for their business, or take on a special role in the group. (For example, "This week you are the teaching assistant. You get to call on boys who have their hands raised to answer a question." Or, "You get to help check everyone's work.") Use your creativity. Boys need to see themselves achieving regularly. Give them lots of feedback opportunities. Ideally, you will give them some things to strive for every week, and then reward them!

Because we are advocating that you think in terms of working with the boys over a period of years, make these Achievement Levels something that takes many months to achieve.

MANHOOD ACHIEVEMENT LEVELS WORKSHEET
LEVEL 1

• Name (what to call it) _____

• What attitudes do we want to see demonstrated? (Examples include showing respect for others; showing that they care about each other; showing that they want to be there by paying attention; showing a willingness to learn and grow; being willing to tell the truth when asked to do so.) _____
_____
_____

• What should their attendance be? _____
_____

• What knowledge do we want them to have at this point? (Examples include knowing the Oath of Manhood; knowing the steps of the Problem Solving Process; knowing how to negotiate or bargain; knowing how to balance a checkbook.) _____
_____
_____
_____

• What behaviors do they need to demonstrate? (These behaviors should be thought of like the Boy Scouts. Examples might include caring for someone, resolving a fight between two people; improving their grades by a certain percent or in a certain area; leading out in prayer at a group meeting; standing before the congregation and reciting the Oath of Manhood.) _____
_____
_____
_____

• What sign of achievement will be used to indicate a boy has reached this level?
_____
_____

• How shall we celebrate a boy's reaching this level? _____
_____
_____

MANHOOD ACHIEVEMENT LEVELS WORKSHEET
LEVEL 2

• Name (what to call it) _____

• What attitudes do we want to see demonstrated? (These attitudes should demonstrate increasing maturity. For example, Level 1 may have asked the boys to listen respectfully when others are talking. Level 2 may ask the boys to take initiative when they see another boy upset, to go to him and comfort him; to pray with him; and to encourage him in some way.) _____

_____

_____

• What should their attendance be? _____

_____

• What knowledge do we want them to have at this point? (This should be knowledge at a more advanced level. Think through what you are teaching them, and then list the most important things they should have learned.) _____

_____

_____

_____

• What behaviors do they need to demonstrate? (These behaviors should show more maturity than the behaviors of Level 1. Think through what you are training them to be. Then write down your expectations for them.) _____

_____

_____

_____

_____

_____

• What sign of achievement will be used to indicate that a boy has reached this level?

_____

• How shall we celebrate a boy's reaching this level? _____

_____

_____

MANHOOD ACHIEVEMENT LEVELS WORKSHEET
LEVEL 3

- Name (what to call it) _____

- What attitudes do we want to see demonstrated? _____
_____
_____
_____

- What should their attendance be? _____
_____
_____
_____

- What knowledge do we want them to have at this point? _____
_____
_____
_____

- What behaviors do they need to demonstrate? _____
_____
_____
_____

- What sign of achievement will be used to indicate a boy has reached this level?
_____
_____
_____
_____

- How shall we celebrate a boy's reaching this level? _____
_____
_____
_____

STRATEGY 6 – CELEBRATE RITES OF PASSAGE RITUALS

So much has been said about rites of passage that we want to say little else except to endorse it as an important strategy. Nathan and Julia Hare's *Bringing the Black Boy to Manhood: The Passage* calls for rituals to help boys know when they have become men in the eyes of their adult community. Our boys today get such rites from their peers – dangerous rites demanded by gangs and other rites such as sexual intercourse. We need to surround our boys with men who hold them to high standards of manhood and then affirm them when they achieve those standards.

The key here is to have rites of passage throughout the program. Don't wait until the end. At each major Achievement Level, and at other times as well, celebrate! African peoples around the world are known for their celebrations in both secular and Christian settings. Achievement Level celebrations are one of the best things you can do to reinforce the months of hard work that you and the boys invest in Project Manhood training. Celebrations are good rewards for the boys and for the trainers, too.

NOTES

_____

_____

_____

_____

_____

_____

_____

_____

_____

_____

_____

_____

INTRODUCTION TO
LET THE JOURNEY BEGIN

Boys cannot raise themselves to be men. They can become adult males, but they will not be authentic men unless someone teaches them what it means to be a man. In traditional Africa, at an appointed time, the boys would be led out of their mothers' homes and out of the village confines by the elders to learn the knowledge, traditions, and practices of adult men. The boys were then initiated into the society of adult men through a rite of passage which would forever imprint upon the young person that now at last he was a man and would be expected to act like one.

But today, no one teaches our boys what it really means to be a man. The result is that many males grow up but are still boys psychologically.

"We hear it said of some man that "he just can't get himself together." A man who "cannot get it together" is a man who has probably not had the opportunity to undergo ritual initiation into the deep structures of manhood. He remains a boy – not because he wants to, but because no one has shown him the way to transform his boy energies into man energies . . . .

"Tribal societies had highly specific notions about adulthood, both masculine and feminine, and how to get to it. And they had ritual processes . . . to enable their children to achieve what we could call calm, secure maturity.

"Our own culture has pseudo-rituals instead . . . . The gangs of our major cities are [a] manifestation of pseudo-initiation, and so are the prison systems, which, in large measure, are run by gangs.

"We call these phenomena pseudo-events . . . [because they] more often than not initiate the boy into a kind of masculinity that is skewed, stunted, and false. It is a patriarchal "manhood," one that is abusive of others, and often of self."

(Moore and Gillette)

Moore and Gillette, Kunjufu, and others agree that the lack of carefully thought through manhood training and rites of passage rituals prevents boys from becoming kings, warriors, etc. This manual provides such training for and initiation into authentic manhood. It is expected to be implemented especially by fathers with their sons. It will create such deep, intensive communication between fathers and their sons that if nothing else happens, the improved relationship between a son and his dad will in itself help him become a better man.

The manual can also be used with a group of boys by a group of men. Indeed, this is an even more powerful way of training the boys (group training is what was used in Africa). This way, you teach not only one boy but also the friends who influence him.

Let the Journey Begin has the following characteristics:

CHRISTIAN VALUES

This manual draws on a theological understanding of manhood which is grounded in Scripture. We believe that there is no "cookie cutter," or single, mold into which all men must fit. On the contrary, God has created tremendously beautiful diversity. We also believe that there are some fundamental characteristics about manhood toward which all men are called by their Creator to strive. In essence, there are some fundamental values, attitudes, habits, and skills which we believe God created men to have. But the personality styles and the many lifestyle choices which face men are between each man and his God. Indeed, we welcome the many different ways men can live as men. But we also assert that there are some core components to manhood which are authored by God.

PRACTICAL

This is not a theoretical book. This is a manual. For 15 to 20 evenings, a father can sit down with his son, or a youth group leader can sit with a group of boys and teach what it means to be a man. The lessons are clearly spelled out, with each step detailed. Of course, a man can make whatever changes or additions he thinks will make the lesson more effective for his boys, but the manual gives him a starting point.

AFROCENTRIC

This manual makes no apologies for focusing boys on their own unique heritage and issues as African Americans. Each module attempts to be faithful to the charge of helping boys develop a pride in their African heritage, but two of the modules in particular will focus the boys on a strong African American identity. Ultimately, to be Afrocentric, a manual must point its students to fight in Christ's name for the full freedom and maturity of African peoples.

CHARACTER AND SKILL FOCUSED

The manual does not spend a lot of time on the problems African Americans face in this country. It is a call to African American boys to seize their own future by developing their character. Such values and attitudes as integrity, competence, ambition, perseverance, toughness, self-discipline, love, and hope are emphasized throughout. So, too, are the mental and social skills which enable a person to live out his values – skills such as problem-solving, planning, decision-making, strategy formulation, positive thinking, active listening, peer resistance, leadership, and effective communication.

STORY BASED

One of the critical ways in which we have failed African American boys is by not giving them a set of stories which can teach the meaning of manhood and a good life. To counter that failure, in *Let the Journey Begin* the Jewish-African story of Joseph is used to give boys an overview of "the road to manhood," a sense of what the journey to adulthood will be like for them. Joseph's story – long identified with by African American people – teaches them about the obstacles they will encounter on the way to authentic manhood and the choices they will have to make. Cut off from the stories passed down from generation to generation in traditional West African societies, the stories which get passed around from teen to teen or from television to teen today lack any larger vision which can help make sense of a boy's life and give him hope and direction for his future. Thus, boys are deeply confused about the meaning of manhood. *Let the Journey Begin* teaches the boys manhood-nourishing and life-affirming stories which can guide them on their journey toward manhood.

In this version, the stories are drawn primarily from the lives and teachings of biblical men. African influences on the Judeo-Christian faith are so numerous and so strong that African peoples in America – and black Africans in Africa – have embraced the Judeo-Christian faith with wholehearted abandon. They have felt understood by this faith and have on subconscious levels recognized their own story in the stories of "the ancient people of God." These have been the primary stories which have affirmed and strengthened African people in America. The retelling of these stories to today's boys can prove a powerful means of guiding them into authentic manhood. It is our hope that somewhere along their journey, the boys will discover the Son of Man and continue their journey with him as their Lord.

Other stories, of course, are drawn from our own African American and African communities. In fact, this manual emphasizes the telling of "Elder Tales." Fathers tell their sons their own life stories. Mentors share incidents from their own lives. Youth group leaders and men from the community share their stories as well. Thus, the boys come to understand in very personal, practical ways what the road to manhood is really like. Carefully selected videos also play a part, as a father, mentor or youth group leaders gets the boys to analyze the meaning of the video stories for their own lives.

BALANCE OF "DISCOVERY LEARNING" AND "DIRECT INSTRUCTION" APPROACHES

It has been said that values are more "caught than taught," while skills are better taught than caught. Educational research reinforces this notion. In the teaching of values and attitudes, there should be an opportunity to kick ideas around. While the stories are presented so that certain values will indeed be learned by the boys, the values are not preached. Rather, they are led to reflect on how those values – or the lack of them – influenced the lives of the characters in the stories as well as how they would influence their own lives and the lives of those around them. Boys need to see the power of these principles for themselves. However, in the learning of skills, lecture and practice are the best means of instruction. So *Let the Journey Begin* utilizes a careful balance between the various teaching methods.

27

This manual, a part of the Project Manhood series, is changing boys' lives. It has been designed by highly trained and experienced African American men whose lives exemplify the principles of authentic manhood taught in this manual. The manual is powerful. It stirs strong emotions in the boys, brings up deep issues, provokes much thought, and powerfully challenges the false beliefs about life and manhood our boys have learned. It does not hesitate to teach principles of manhood which the team has gathered from many disciplines, including psychology, history, sociology, social work, the ministry, education, and African American studies – in all of which members of the team have had long training and experience.

Men using this manual with boys should be prepared to study carefully the recommended background reading, attend training seminars, and be involved in a men's group themselves. All of us involved with Project Manhood, including the authors, have had our own notions of manhood challenged and ultimately strengthened. We are better men for the experience, and you will be also. The boys will make sure of that.

Finally, men using this manual should be prepared for deep feelings to surface in the boys, many evenings spent contending with deep attitudes of inferiority, irresponsibility, hopelessness, ignorance, and false machismo. Our boys do not come easily into manhood. This society has seen to that by placing many obstacles and traumas in their path.

As a father or mentor, you must see your role as one of:

PROTECTOR,
shielding your boy from the lies he will be told about being a man and the "false manhood traps" that lie in wait for him along the road to adulthood;

TEACHER,
guiding him into the truth that the Enemy will attempt to keep from him;

MOTIVATOR,
helping him not to give up in the face of the many obstacles in his path. This manual will help you do this.

If you are a youth group leader, you must commit not to a program, but to a generation of boys for six to twelve years until they are safely through the dangerous adolescent years and have become solid young African American men.

We wish you all of the courage, wisdom, patience, perseverance, and love that you will need to overcome what has been done to our boys and to lead them onto the road to authentic manhood. We stand ready to help you in whatever way we can. Do not hesitate to write us at:

Project Manhood
Renaissance Productions
537 Mantua Avenue – Suite 203
Woodbury, NJ 08096

FOR FATHERS

If you are a father who has decided to really teach your son how to be a man, we congratulate you. You cannot know now how much tragedy you will help your son avoid in his life by doing this.

But we also warn you. You will encounter the "Father Wound." This is the wound we must all face if we are to become the men God wants us to be. The Father Wound is the hurt and pain you yourself feel, and which your son now feels on some level, because neither of you had perfect fathers. The Father Wound is all the things you did not learn from your father (nor your son from you) because fathers are so often absent physically or emotionally. They are "out there" working, working out, relaxing, womanizing, or doing something other than loving, teaching, and nurturing their sons in an open and consistent manner.

Don't be overly concerned about this Father Wound. If you are uncertain exactly how to raise your son, you are like most of us. What you need is some assistance in how to do it. *Let the Journey Begin* provides you with some of that assistance. For 15 to 20 evenings, you and your son can have an intensive time of biblical study, discussion, watching videos, talking with other men, and kicking ideas around about what this journey to man-

hood is all about. He will never forget these sessions with you. Nor will you. Your reward will be to see your relationship with your son deepen, even if you don't live with him. You will also see him wrestle with some principles that can make his life so much more fulfilling than it will be if he never has anyone to bring these principles to him for his consideration.

We encourage you to see this as a sharing time with your son rather than a preaching time. You can share your values and your life story with him without trying to make him accept what you say. Just as importantly, encourage him as much as possible to share his own perspectives and feelings. DON'T BE DEFENSIVE OR ANGRY AT HIS FEELINGS. He has been mis-educated in many ways about what being a man is about – and he is different from you. He needs time to develop his own thoughts about things. Give him that time – time with you and with other men you respect, time to bounce his thoughts off you and to think things through. Pray for him, and trust that along his life's journey he will hear and answer God's call to true manhood.

Keep in mind that you don't have to be perfect to teach him. You just have to be growing yourself and wrestling with the same issues. That will be good enough to help your son further along his road toward authentic manhood.

Finally, you should consider inviting your son's friends – or asking him to invite them – into your sessions, so that you can reach the boys who influence him. You might even suggest co-teaching this curriculum with the fathers of your son's friends. If you do this, you are then leading a group and might benefit from the following guidelines.

FOR YOUTH GROUP LEADERS

This manual can be utilized by one man with one boy or by a group of men with a group of boys. If you are working with three or more boys, please follow these guidelines:

1. FORM A STRONG GROUP CONSCIOUSNESS.
Boys, especially our boys, are powerfully drawn to groups (hence the power of gangs). Your task as a group leader is to form these boys into a group twice as powerful as the gangs which may be attempting to recruit them. They should become proud to be a part of this group. Give the group a name which will make them proud, just as the gangs do. We recommend that you choose an African or biblical name, either of which will draw on the powerful cultural images which were discussed above and begin to help them identify with the proper images of manhood.

2. MAINTAIN PROPER GROUP SIZE, MEETING FREQUENCY, AND DISCIPLINE.
Groups should be no larger than 20. They should meet at least once per week. On the night the manual is to be used, you will generally need TWO HOURS.

Let the Journey Begin is a highly structured time. Besides this highly structured, intense session, however, the boys also need times to have more free-flowing discussions (rap times) about various subjects, and time for physical activities and other exercise which challenge their sense of manhood. Thus, it would be helpful to have two meetings per week so that they can get both structure and freedom.

Discipline should be maintained fairly strictly at all times. While it may seem harsh, the boys are crying out for sensitive discipline. Rules should be posted and should include:

1. RESPECT EVERYONE: No name calling.

2. USE PROPER LANGUAGE: No cursing.

3. DEMONSTRATE COMMITMENT: No unexcused absences.

4. HANDLE CONFLICTS AS A MAN: No unfair fighting.

5. MAINTAIN SECRETS: What is told in the group stays in the group.

6. PERSEVERE: No giving up.

Violations of these rules should be dealt with since they destroy the cohesiveness and viability of the group. DO NOT SHAME the boys when applying discipline. Treat them with respect and as "men-under-construction." But be consistent and firm about these rules. On the whole, despite the intensity, the manual gently leads them toward proper attitudes. Therefore, be firm with the basic rules.

3. BALANCE STRUCTURE WITH FREEDOM.
As mentioned earlier, the manual is highly structured. It has specific things which the trainer must say to the boys, do with the boys, and get the boys to talk about. These "lecturettes" and exercises have been very carefully thought through and tested, and it is important to do them as written. At the same time, no two trainers are the same and no two groups of boys are the same. Therefore, if additional time is needed on a given week to deal with certain things which come up or with closely related issues that the trainer wants the boys to follow up on, this is permissible. We call these "Village Talks." Be careful, however, not to lose the focus of the manual. If extended time is needed to deal with these issues, schedule them for a second session of the week, or a Saturday workshop.

Also, in some cases it will not be possible to finish a lesson in one meeting. The lesson should simply be picked up at the next session, with an appropriate summary of what was learned, preferably given by the boys themselves as a means to reinforce learning.

4. FOLLOW UP WITH INDIVIDUAL TIME WITH THE BOYS.
As mentioned earlier, this training program evokes deep feelings in the boys and much intense discussion. It is important that when the trainer senses a boy is struggling with something or is on the verge of a breakthrough in some area, he should get with the boy individually to follow up. It may also involve getting with the family since a lot of what the boys talk about is their families. Social work or case management may also be included where these are available. It is important for the trainer to know his skills, and not to go beyond them. If he is not trained or skilled in counseling, deeper emotional struggles and family dysfunctionality should be referred to appropriate professionals.

VILLAGE TALK

5. USE MEN ONLY.
Women have a crucial role to play in the rearing of our boys. But everything we know about getting boys fully into adulthood as authentic men says that at some point in

their lives they must come into the man's world and learn from men what it means to be an adult man. Women can tell boys about manhood, but only men can show them. It has only been in the past few decades that this principle has been questioned because of the increasing dysfunctionality of many African American men and because of women's understandable concerns about finding appropriate male role models.

Nonetheless, *Let the Journey Begin* presents an opportunity to bring reasonably mature adult male role models into a boy's life, and this should not be sacrificed. He will never forget the experience of finding a man he can look up to who can teach him about manhood, put his arm around him, and make him feel special. What we ask of women is to affirm the budding masculinity of the boys in the group and to affirm the adult males who are teaching them. At Project Manhood, we give various suggestions for how women can take a rest, let men teach the boys, and support both boys and men.

6. GIVE PREFERENCE TO AFRICAN AMERICAN MEN.

Since *Let the Journey Begin* and Project Manhood are Afrocentric, it is critical that the primary leadership in the program be by African American men. Men of other races can play an important supportive role in training and mentoring the boys. But the boys should be able to look up to African American men as the primary leaders for their own self-esteem and for the proper functioning of the program.

MATERIALS NEEDED

• Video cassette player (Sessions 1, 10)
• Video: *Glory* (Session 1)
• Video: *Chariots of Fire* (or other appropriate video about not giving up in the face of difficulty) (Session 10)
• This manual for each mentor
• A student handbook for each boy
• Newsprint and/or chalkboard (for groups)
• A pack of plant seeds (enough for each boy to receive a seed) (Session 5)
• *Forgive & Forget* (paperback book by Lewis Smedes, Pocket Books). Order enough for each mentor and each boy to purchase a copy (Session 12)
• A gift to be given to each boy during the Rite of Passage celebration. The gift should be a symbol of what it means to be a man. You will have to look around and see what is available. You want them to remember their Oath whenever they look at the gift. (Session 16)

CONVENTIONS USED IN THIS CURRICULUM

Mentors will find cues at the left side of each column suggesting an effective way to control the flow of discussions. A series of questions will be introduced with a heading such as *Ask* or *Say*. For each question, the boys are to volunteer answers from their reading or from their experience. We put suggested answers in italic type following each question to simplify your preparation for each session.

LET THE JOURNEY BEGIN — CURRICULUM

The call to manhood comes at different times in each boy's life. Perhaps it comes when an older boy picks a fight with the boy. For some it comes when gangs start approaching them. For others, it comes when the father leaves the home or the boy discovers that his father has children by another woman. Sometimes it comes at puberty.

The boy does not recognize it as a call to "manhood," but that is what it is. It is a call to grow up, to put childhood behind, and to embrace adult values, attitudes, and skills. This first stage in the Project Manhood Series is designed to help a boy recognize that he has been called (he will come to discover that the call comes from God) to become a man.

The call to manhood is a call to undertake the hero's journey. The path is the path of the hero who, fundamentally, is called out of his limited world as he knows it to face many challenges through which he grows strong, wise, and loving and then returns to the community he left to call others to maturity and freedom. Joseph Campbell, in his classic study *The Hero with a Thousand Faces,* outlines the typical stages of the hero's jour-

ney found in stories from around the world. Same hero idea, but a thousand different names and faces.

The Jewish-African story of Joseph in Egypt simply but effectively charts the journey Campbell traces and is used as the primary framework for the lessons. You should use it constantly to orient yourself and the boys with whom you are working.

This curriculum encourages boys to enter the road to manhood. Its essential goal is to help them understand what the journey will be like and to motivate them to take the journey. It will help them understand that there are obstacles on the path of every man under construction and to understand that it is their task to overcome these obstacles and win the battle to become a man.

By giving boys a sense that their lives are heroic, that they are caught up in a great struggle between good and evil, and that they are called to fight on the side of good, their self-esteem will be raised and they will take their own lives more seriously. Going to school will be seen as part of the hero's quest for knowledge. Dealing with family dynamics and dysfunctionality will be seen as part of the hero's background. He must take what he can, discard the rest, and then depart to a new land of adulthood. Dealing with his own internal feelings and confusion will be seen as the hero's normal, natural struggle to find his inner strength, clarity, and power.

Psychologist Victor Frankl, in his classic *Man's Search for Meaning,* drawn from his experiences in the concentration camps of Hitler's Germany, shows clearly that the people who did best in those horrible conditions (as best as possible under the circumstances; there were not many choices) were those who could put their suffering into a larger framework – those who chose to give

their suffering a larger meaning. They saw themselves as having something to live for, something worth fighting for. It is this sense of having something worth fighting for which *Let the Journey Begin* seeks to give the boys. Joseph, like all heroes, went through tremendous trials and struggles, but his sense of having something worth fighting for (in his case a sense of integrity rooted in faith in his God and God's call on his life) is what carried him through.

So many of our boys today do not know how to suffer, how to endure, how to persevere, and how to excel in the face of obstacles. They must be taught to suffer properly, and that only comes when they see themselves as heroes on a journey we all must take.

IN SEARCH OF GLORY

This session motivates the boys to strive toward authentic manhood by depicting life as a hero's journey. The purpose is to begin to focus the boys on the development of their character.

GOALS

At the end of this session, the boys will be able to:
1. State clearly that life is a battle and that the world needs them to be heroes.
2. State that the central test of being a hero is the development of a character which can face and overcome serious challenges to their manhood.
3. State that they need each other and a power beyond themselves to win the battle.

MATERIALS NEEDED

• Video cassette player • Video: *Glory*
• This manual • Student workbooks
• Bibles • The Oath of Manhood • The Road to Manhood map • Newsprint or chalkboard (for groups)

WARM UP

1. Have your boys recite the Oath of Manhood (page 39 and on the back cover of the boys' activity book). You may end in a prayer for learning and growth or a moment of quiet meditation on what they want to get out of this session.

FATHERS/MENTORS:
Recite the Oath with your boys.

2. Create a sense of mystery and excitement by asking the boys to sit quietly with the lights dim. Do not answer any questions about what video they will be watching. Pause dramatically for a quiet moment. Tell them to take a minute to either think or pray (their choice) about what kind of man they want to be.

OPENING ACTIVITY
(2 hours 30 minutes)

FATHERS/MENTORS:
While this activity can be done with one man and one boy, it would be better to invite at least one other boy over, especially since you will show a video. The other activities in the curriculum can be done effectively either with one boy or with a group of boys. However, on some occasions, different activities are suggested for Fathers than for Mentors.

SHOW:
Glory video. Stop the video at three places and lead discussion as follows:

STOP 1:

Scene: The Sergeant Major is drilling the troops. Col. Shaw tells him to come over and asks him if he is being a bit hard on the troops. The following exchange takes place:

> Sergeant Major: "The boy's your friend, is he?"

> Col. Shaw: "We grew up together, yes."

> Sergeant Major: "Let him grow up some more."

STOP THE FILM HERE!

ASK:

1. "What is motivating these men to be soldiers? Why do they want to be soldiers?" Let the boys answer without commenting on their answers other than acknowledging them.

> • *Answers include: To be free to demonstrate "courage, spirit, and honor" as Col. Shaw puts it; "pride and dignity to those who have known only degradation," as Frederick Douglass puts it in the video.*

2. "What kept them there the next morning after the threat was made by the Confederate States that any blacks caught in uniform would be killed immediately?"

> • *After they have expressed their answers, emphasize that the men's desire to achieve their goal is greater than their fear of death.*

3. "Can you think of anyone who risked death for his goal?"

> ***Biblical/Religious Characters:***
> *a. Moses, when he went before Pharaoh and demanded in God's name that Pharaoh let the Jews go free.*
> *b. Daniel, when he refused to pray to the king and he was thrown into the lions' den.*
> *c. Gideon, who went with just 300 men to attack thousands of Philistines.*
> *d. The Apostle Paul, who risked death many times to preach the gospel.*
> *e. Mohammed, who developed a new and controversial religion.*

> ***Characters from African American History:***
> *a. Denmark Vesey, who led a slave mutiny.*
> *b. Sojourner Truth, who led many slaves to freedom.*
> *c. Frederick Douglass, who spoke for African slaves among the powerful of white America.*
> *d. Martin Luther King, Jr., who risked death many times to lead the Civil Rights Movement and who was finally killed.*

4. "What does the sergeant major mean when he tells Col. Shaw, 'Let him grow up some more?'"

> • *The man needs to add to his life not only academic and intellectual ability, but also toughness and strength in the midst of difficulty. He must find his inner strength and not just rely on his friend, Robert.*

BREAK

(15 minutes)

If a break is going to be taken, this is the best place to do it, before the story and discussion have become too intense.

SHOW:
Resume showing the video.

STOP 2:
Scene: After the whipping scene, where a soldier is whipped supposedly for desertion, the older soldier, Mr. Rollins, tells Col. Shaw that the man had been out looking for shoes. Stop the tape after the scene in the tent where they take off the whipped man's shoes, showing his scarred back.

ASK:
1. "The men have been getting armed with guns, receiving shoes, learning to fight with bayonets, and learning to re-load while being shot at. What do you need to be armed with to be prepared to fight your battles? What training do you need?"

2. "In what ways were these soldiers tested as men? What challenges did they face as they prepared for battle?"

a. Bayonet scene: Thomas had to grow up some more. When he was down and defeated, he couldn't rely on Col. Shaw, but had to find strength within himself.

b. Tent scene where one man is bullying the others: The soldier, Trip, taunted Thomas about thinking he was so smart. Trip valued street smarts more than edu-

cation. How often do kids who drop out of school taunt those who stay in school? Thomas had to learn a new set of skills without throwing away his old set. He needed to keep his book learning and yet learn soldiering. We, too, need to be both street smart and book learned.

c. Whipping scene: Even though Trip was unjustly whipped, he still wanted to be a soldier. We have to learn to persevere even when we are treated unjustly. We cannot let other people's injustice get us off track.

STOP 3:
End of the video.

ASK:
"What does this video tell us about being a hero? What is essential about being a man?"

a. At the end as he volunteered the 54th to attack the fort and the General was questioning whether the men would be too tired to lead the attack, Col. Shaw said, "There's more to fighting than rest, Sir. There's character. There's strength of heart."

b. Being a hero, a real man, is more about your strength of character than your strength of muscle. They also had to learn to count on each other and on their faith in God.

COMMITMENT

(3 minutes)

ASK:
Ask your boys to quietly identify one area of their character which needs to grow.

Have them write the answer in their workbook.

> • *Courage, toughness, being willing to risk and sacrifice to achieve a goal, and being a man of your word.*

COMMIT:
Have boys stand and quietly commit to themselves and to God to grow in that area.

The Oath of Manhood

Eight Attitudes Authentic Men Have

Attitude	Meaning	Basis*
1 — I am Teachable	I am strong enough to know that I need help. I need the Lord and I need other people.	Blessed are the poor in spirit, for theirs is the kingdom of heaven.
2 — I am Determined	Pain doesn't make me give up. It makes me grow.	Blessed are those who mourn, for they will be comforted.
3 — I am a Gentleman	I am assertive like Christ, not aggressive. I always treat everyone with respect.	Blessed are the meek, for they will inherit the earth.
4 — I am Principled	I make choices based on my principles and goals, striving for moral integrity & personal excellence.	Blessed are those who hunger and thirst for righteousness, for they will be filled.
5 — I am Loving	I try to love others the way that Jesus Christ has loved me, seeking their highest good.	Blessed are the merciful, for they will be shown mercy.
6 — I am Open-Hearted & Open-Minded	I am not defensive. I have opened myself deeply to God's truth, and He gives me wisdom in everything I face.	Blessed are the pure in heart, for they will see God.
7 — I am a Bridge Builder	I try to understand others and find win-win solutions to problems.	Blessed are the peace-makers, for they will be called children of God.
8 — I am a Warrior	I fight for justice & true freedom for my people, with Christ's power pulling down the strongholds that hold them captive.	Blessed are those who are persecuted because of righteousness, for theirs is the kingdom of heaven.

I AM AN AFRICAN AMERICAN MAN OF GOD.

*Taken from Matthew 5:3–10.

NOTES

CALL TO MANHOOD— CHOOSING YOUR DESTINY

This session introduces a boy to the difference that choice – responsibility – can make in his life. So many of our boys have no sense of the ability to make any real difference in their lives. Psychologists call it a sense of "efficacy," a sense that you can make choices and achieve certain effects in your life. You are responsible for what you choose and for the consequences. This session teaches boys that they must choose to become authentic men. They must choose to take the road to authentic manhood and stay on it.

GOALS

At the end of this session, your boys will be able to:
1. Understand the concepts of "choice" and "responsibility."
2. Grasp the life-long importance of the choices they make today.
3. Commit to making the choices that lead to authentic manhood.

MATERIALS NEEDED

- This manual • Student workbooks
- Bibles • The Oath of Manhood
- The Road to Manhood map

WARM UP

1. Have your boys recite the Oath of Manhood p. 39. You may end in a prayer for learning and growth or a moment of quiet meditation on what they want to get out of this session. **FATHERS/MENTORS:** Recite the Oath with your boys.

VILLAGE TALK

2. Village Talk: This time is to provide boys with an opportunity to talk about the ways they have experienced various aspects of their manhood training since the last meeting.

OPENING ACTIVITY THE POWER OF CHOICE

ELDER TALE:
Tell your boys a story of a choice you made at some point in your life and the effects of that choice on your life. It would be good if the choice you made had a long-lasting effect so that your boys

can understand that there are sometimes long-term consequences to what they choose.

FOR GROUPS

It would be good if you had several men share choices they have made, some good and some bad. This way, the boys have more examples to help them understand the power of choice.

READ:
Have the boys take turns reading Daniel 1:1-20.

EXPLAIN:
"Daniel lived at a time when the Babylonian King Nebuchadnezzar was invading Judah, where the Jews lived. Nebuchadnezzar defeated the Jewish army at Jerusalem, captured many of the boys, and had them sent back to him in Babylon. There they lived in King Nebuchadnezzar's palace and served him."

ASK:
1. "How does Daniel 1:3 and 4 describe the young men the king wanted? What kind of young men did the king want?" (If your boys don't notice some parts of the description, direct them to appropriate portions of the story and ask them leading questions. This way, you are helping them with reading comprehension as you cover the topic.)
- *They were to be from the royal family and nobility and were to be without any physical defect, handsome, showing aptitude for every kind of learning, well informed, quick to understand, and qualified to serve in the king's palace.*

2. "What did King Nebuchadnezzar want them to do?"
- *To be taught the language and literature of the Babylonians.*
- *To eat food and wine from the king's table. This was considered to be the best food in Babylon. The king wanted his captives to be strong and healthy so they could work for him.*
- *To be trained for three years in all the skills and knowledge they would need to serve in the king's court.*
- *After their training, to take up various positions in Nebuchadnezzar's palace.*

3. "What choice did Daniel make in Daniel 1:8?"
- *Not to defile himself – not to make himself unholy before God – by eating the king's food.*

EXPLAIN:
"The king's food was food used in the Babylonian religions. By eating the food, Daniel would have made it seem that he was now accepting the religions of the Babylonians. Sometimes you may hang out with some boys who are doing something wrong, and you may not be doing it. But the fact that you are there while they are doing it makes it seem like you, too, are doing wrong. It's better to just stay away from them, at least while they are doing something wrong. That is what Daniel did. Daniel didn't want anyone to think he was doing anything wrong. So he asked to keep away from their food, to be allowed to eat the food that God said he should eat."

ASK:

1. "What was the reaction of the man the king had put over Daniel and his friends (Daniel 1:9)?"

> • *He was afraid of the king's reaction. He knew the king wanted the men to be healthy and strong. If they didn't eat the food the king was offering – which was the best food in Babylon, he thought – then Daniel and his friends wouldn't look as healthy as the other young men, and the official would get into trouble.*

2. "What solution did Daniel propose in verses 11-13?"

> • *That the man give Daniel and his friends the kind of food God wanted them to eat and test them in ten days to see if they looked better than the other young men who were eating the Babylonian food.*

3. "What was the result of this test (Daniel 1:15)?"

> • *Daniel and his friends looked healthier and better nourished than the other boys.*

4. "What did God do for Daniel and his three friends because they made the choice to be faithful to what He had told them to do?"

> • *God gave them knowledge and understanding of all kinds of literature and learning. He made them A+ students. He also gave Daniel the ability to understand dreams and visions.*

5. "What can we say, then, about how important are the choices you make as a young man?"

> • *Very important. They will determine how healthy you will be, how good a life you will have, and how many blessings God will give you. If you want to be a good student and have a good life, you have to make the right choices.*

SAY:

"This is what the men in the video *Glory* had to do. They had to make the choice to go into battle, even if they might die. It was the only way they could get the respect of the white men who thought that blacks could not make good soldiers. Even though they were afraid, they chose to fight."

> • *In your life, you have to learn to make the right choices so that God can make you a strong and wise man like He did Daniel and his buddies.*

BREAK

(15 minutes for groups)

EXERCISE: THE POWER OF MY CHOICES

Have the boys open their workbooks to "The Power of My Choices." Have them fill out the exercise, and then discuss it with them.

FATHERS:

This is an opportunity for you to teach your values to your son. Invite him to discuss his perspectives with you. Ask him what he thinks the consequences might be if he makes the wrong or right decision concerning the choice he now has to make. Ask him what he thinks he needs to consider in making this decision. Help him understand how you see the choice he is facing, but don't preach! Just quietly share the way you see it.

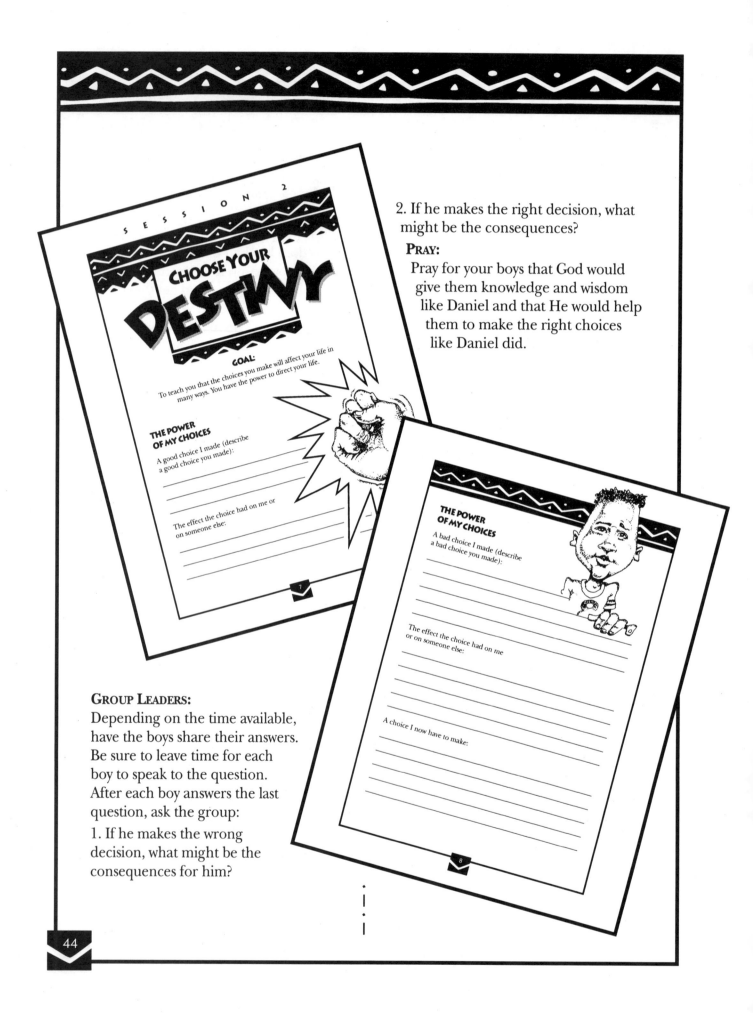

SESSION 2

CHOOSE YOUR DESTINY

GOAL:

To teach you that the choices you make will affect your life in many ways. You have the power to direct your life.

THE POWER OF MY CHOICES

A good choice I made (describe a good choice you made):

_____

_____

The effect the choice had on me or on someone else:

_____

_____

7

THE POWER OF MY CHOICES

A bad choice I made (describe a bad choice you made):

_____

_____

The effect the choice had on me or on someone else:

_____

_____

A choice I now have to make:

_____

_____

8

2. If he makes the right decision, what might be the consequences?

PRAY:

Pray for your boys that God would give them knowledge and wisdom like Daniel and that He would help them to make the right choices like Daniel did.

GROUP LEADERS:

Depending on the time available, have the boys share their answers. Be sure to leave time for each boy to speak to the question. After each boy answers the last question, ask the group:

1. If he makes the wrong decision, what might be the consequences for him?

FIRST CHALLENGE—FAMILY STRENGTHS AND WEAKNESSES

This session begins to help your boys to identify the challenges they will face as they journey toward manhood. It is clear from Scripture and from experience that for a person to become a true man, he must come to grips with what he has learned and experienced in his family. He must try to understand how he was influenced and continue to affirm what he learned that was positive, leaving behind what was negative. He must make up his own mind about things.

"Mama's got hers. . . . Papa's got his. . . . but God bless the child that's got his own," to paraphrase the old song. The Bible puts a more positive emphasis on it, "Therefore a man shall leave his father and his mother . . ." (Genesis 2:24, NKJV). Leaving and putting "childish ways behind" us (I Corinthians 13:11, NKJV) is a major challenge. In this session, boys will begin to learn to sort out their feelings about their families. As they get older, they will develop more and more ability to think through issues carefully and to make up their own minds.

This session invites boys to share about hurts they may have experienced in order to begin to move toward healing. Leaders may want to inform parents of your purpose and direction. In addition, be alert to refer families to competent professionals if issues arise which are beyond your expertise.

GOALS

At the end of this session, your boys will be able to:
1. Identify some of the strengths in their family and some of the problems.
2. Understand that they should build on what has been helpful about their families and change what has been hurtful.
3. State specifically to their father or mother what they appreciate and what they would like changed. This will help promote intimate communication between parents and son.

MATERIALS NEEDED

• This manual • Student workbooks
• Bibles • The Oath of Manhood
• The Road to Manhood map
• Newsprint or chalkboard

WARM UP

1. Have your boys recite the Oath of Manhood. End in a prayer for learning and growth. **FATHERS/MENTORS:** Recite the Oath with your boys.

VILLAGE TALK

2. Village Talk: This time is to provide boys with an opportunity to talk about the ways they have experienced various aspects of their manhood training since the last meeting.

Trainers should briefly review the key points of the prior manhood training session. Trainers should also bring various visual aids (pictures, news articles, stories, quotes, etc.) that will help boys to focus on key points of prior and current training sessions.

OPENING ACTIVITY: NAME THIS PERSON

Do:
Ask each boy to stand up and imitate someone in his family (father, mother, sister, brother, grandmother, etc.) without naming that person. He can imitate the person's saying something he likes to hear or something he doesn't like to hear. Tell him to really try to sound like the person, including gestures.

Group Leaders:
As each boy imitates someone in his family, have the other boys guess who it is. Make sure each boy gets his opportunity. Feel free to imitate someone in your family if you like.

Fathers/Mentors:
Try to guess who the boy is imitating. Then you imitate someone in your family and let the boy guess. You can do two or three rounds of this if you like.

EXPLORATION

Say:
"Today we are going to begin to explore the challenges you are going to have to overcome on your way to manhood. Becoming a man is not easy. There are many, many obstacles and challenges you are going to face. One of them is your family. Some of the things you are experiencing as you grow up are giving you a good foundation for the future. But I know and you know that some of what you are experiencing with your family is not always easy for you to deal with. Every family has its good and bad aspects, and the challenge you have to face as a man will be to make up your own mind about what your parents taught you. Some of it you will want to hold on to. Some of it you may decide you want to do differently. That's okay. That's what it means to be a man – making up your own mind about how you want to live your life.

"So right now we are going to look at how you see your family."

Read:
Have the boys take turns reading Genesis 37:1-36.

Ask:
1. "Joseph and his family were experiencing family problems. What were they?" List them on newsprint as your boys say

them. If your boys don't notice some problems, direct them to the relevant portion of the story and ask them leading questions. This way, you help them with reading comprehension as you cover the topic. The curriculum uses the story format quite a bit, so they need to learn to analyze a story.

> • *Favoritism by his father; death of his mother; anger, and even hatred from his half brothers because they were hurt and jealous; brothers got rid of him; brothers lied to their father.*

2. "Why did Joseph's brothers hate him?"

> • *Because they were hurt and jealous from their father's showing favoritism toward Joseph. (The "coat of many colors" was a sign of being special. People who wore such coats did not work in the fields because the coats were long and would catch in the bushes. Thus, Joseph seemed not to have to do the kind of hard field work his brothers had to do.)*

> • *Because Joseph told their father a bad report about them. This rubbed them the wrong way, even if they were wrong. Here they were working hard, and Joseph told on them.*

> • *Because Joseph had dreams that made him seem above them.*

> • *Because Joseph was insensitive to his brothers' feelings and kept telling them his dreams, even though they didn't like it; Joseph didn't seem to even notice that they hated him.*

3. "What do you think Joseph learned from his father that was good – that would help him as he journeyed through life?"

> • *Faith in his father's God.*

> • *Self-confidence and self-esteem. Joseph went overboard, but we do need to feel good about ourselves.*

> • *A strong commitment to his family. Joseph never forgot about them or stopped caring for them.*

BREAK
(15 minutes for groups)

EXERCISE:
MY FAMILY PICTURE ALBUM

This is the time to let your boys discuss their own family situation. Have them turn in their workbook to "My Family Picture Album." Explain that a picture album is where we put pictures we have taken so that we can go back to look at them later. The Family Picture Album your boys are about to do will help them look at some things about their own family.

DISCUSS:
Ask your boys to share their answers to the Family Picture Album. Encourage them to talk freely. Focus on their making the distinction between what has been helpful and what has been hurtful. Help them realize that they will want to build on what has been helpful and find ways to change what they've learned that has been hurtful.

GROUP LEADERS:
Be sure to stop immediately any boy who laughs, teases, or makes other trust-breaking responses. This is critical. Be firm and immediate. You must communicate through your firmness that this

group is going to be a safe place for the boys to open up.

EXERCISE: MY PARENTS AND ME

Have the boys turn to the "My Parents and Me" exercise in their workbook. One by one, go through each "C," explaining it to the boys and having them put an X where they feel their parent is. The Cs are Closeness, Communication, Control, Checking Up, Cash, and Christ. If they have a father in the house or one they see often, have them think in terms of their father. If their father is absent or not around much, have them think in terms of their mother or other primary guardian.

GROUP LEADERS:
Tally the answers on newsprint so all the boys can see where everyone put an X. One way to do this is to write out ahead of time all the Cs, with the lines below them, and have each boy put an X on the newsprint line exactly where he put an X in his own workbook.

EXERCISE: DEAR DAD/MOM

Have your boys turn to the "Dear Dad/Mom" exercise in their workbook. Ask them to write a letter to their Dad if he is in the house or if they see him often. (If you are the father, they should still do the exercise!) Otherwise, they should write it to their mother or guardian as before. Then have them copy the letter they wrote onto a blank sheet of paper so they can give it to their parent and still keep in their workbooks a record of what they wrote.

GROUP LEADERS SAY:
Some of you shared some real pain that you are experiencing in your families. As you can see from the Joseph story, guys will experience pain in life. As we read more of his story and other stories, you will discover that you can overcome your family struggles and live a fulfilling, happy life. We are going to teach you the

MY PARENT AND ME

Put an X at the position on the line that says how you feel about your father (or mother if father isn't around) and you.

CLOSENESS: The degree to which my father/mother expresses affection for me.

Physical Hugs

| Never | Sometimes | Often | All the time |

Words of Love

| Never | Sometimes | Often | All the time |

COMMUNICATION: The communication between my father/mother and me.

My father/mother listens to me respectfully:

| Never | Sometimes | Often | All the time |

I listen to my father/mother respectfully:

| Never | Sometimes | Often | All the time |

CONTROL: My father/mother allows me to make my own decisions?

| Never | Sometimes | Often | All the time |

CHECKING UP: My dad knows what I am doing.

Checks up on my school work

| Never | Sometimes | Often | All the time |

Checks up on who my friends are and what I do with them

| Never | Sometimes | Often | All the time |

CASH: My dad gives me money.

| Never | Sometimes | Often | All the time |

CHRIST: My dad teaches me about Jesus.

| Never | Sometimes | Often | All the time |

10

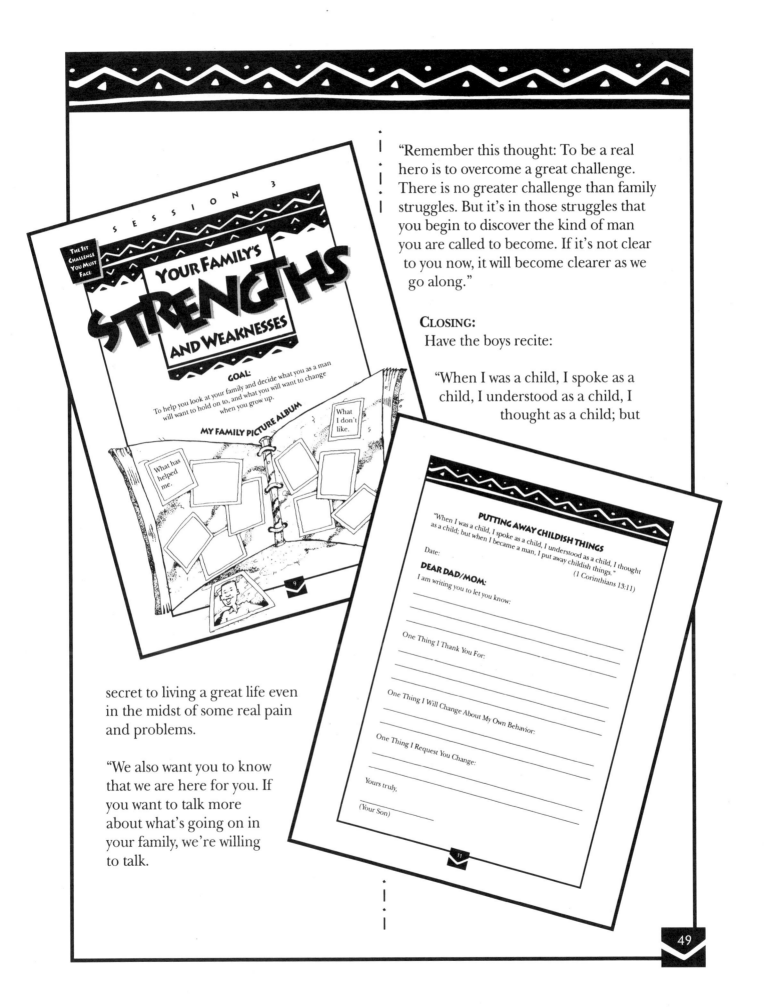

SESSION 3

THE 1ST CHALLENGE YOU MUST FACE

YOUR FAMILY'S STRENGTHS AND WEAKNESSES

GOAL:

To help you look at your family and decide what you as a man will want to hold on to, and what you will want to change when you grow up.

MY FAMILY PICTURE ALBUM

What I don't like.

What has helped me.

9

"Remember this thought: To be a real hero is to overcome a great challenge. There is no greater challenge than family struggles. But it's in those struggles that you begin to discover the kind of man you are called to become. If it's not clear to you now, it will become clearer as we go along."

CLOSING:

Have the boys recite:

"When I was a child, I spoke as a child, I understood as a child, I thought as a child; but

secret to living a great life even in the midst of some real pain and problems.

"We also want you to know that we are here for you. If you want to talk more about what's going on in your family, we're willing to talk.

PUTTING AWAY CHILDISH THINGS

"When I was a child, I spoke as a child, I understood as a child, I thought as a child; but when I became a man, I put away childish things."

(1 Corinthians 13:11)

Date: _____

DEAR DAD/MOM:

I am writing you to let you know:

_____
_____

One Thing I Thank You For:

_____
_____

One Thing I Will Change About My Own Behavior:

_____
_____

One Thing I Request You Change:

_____
_____

Yours truly,

_____
(Your Son)

11

when I became a man, I put away childish things" (I Corinthians 13:11, NKJV).

SAY:

"Remember, nobody's parents are perfect. No one has a perfect family. You are going to have to take the helps and change (or put away) the hurts you don't agree with. A man has to put childish ways of living and thinking behind him, even if he learned them from his family. As you grow up, you will have more and more responsibility for your own life.

Learn to think carefully now about how you want to live."

FATHERS:

Tell your boy that you will read carefully his letter to you, think about what he has said about your family, and get back to him about what changes you plan to make. Thank him for being honest with you, and encourage him to come talk to you at any time about his perceptions of the family.

NOTES

_____

_____

_____

_____

_____

_____

_____

_____

_____

_____

_____

_____

SECOND CHALLENGE—YOUR CHARACTER

This session continues to help boys identify the challenges they face on their way toward authentic manhood. The second challenge is understanding the areas of their character which need to grow and develop. An uncontrolled temper, a passive attitude, poor self-esteem, unresolved anger, a tendency to procrastinate, short attention span – these are just some possible character traits which your boys may need to work on.

Your task in this session is to help your boys identify the areas of growth they currently need to focus on and to make a commitment to grow in those areas. If they begin now the vital habits of self-examination and working to grow, they will be less likely to go far off the track as they get older. A habit of self-honesty – what we call being "open hearted" – is an essential part of being an authentic man.

GOALS

At the end of this session, your boys will be able to:
1. Understand the concepts of "character" and "growth areas."
2. Identify their own character growth areas.
3. Commit to working on their growth areas.

MATERIALS NEEDED

• This manual • Student workbooks • Bibles • The Oath of Manhood • The Road to Manhood map • Newsprint or chalkboard

WARM UP

1. Have your boys recite the Oath of Manhood. You may end in a prayer for learning and growth or a moment of quiet meditation on what they want to get out of this session. **FATHERS/MENTORS:** Recite the Oath with your boy.

VILLAGE TALK

2. Village Talk: Ask the boys how they have been doing with their families and if any of them received any response from the letter they gave their father. Keep this short. You can say things like, "That sounds difficult. We will probably talk more about that kind of problem in future sessions." If there is a lot of pain, you may need to spend the rest of the ses-

sion dealing with it. You will then have to reschedule this session. Don't try to do both an extended discussion of family problems and this session.

OPENING ACTIVITY: JOSEPH'S CHARACTER GROWTH AREAS

READ:

Have the boys take turns reading Genesis 37:1-36.

REVIEW:

1. "Last time, what did we say were Joseph's family problems?" (List them on newsprint as the boys say them. As you did last time, if they don't notice some problems, direct them to the appropriate portion of the story and ask leading questions. This way, you help them with reading comprehension as you cover the topic.)

> • *Favoritism by his father; death of his mother (which happens before this scene opens); anger and even hatred from his half brothers because they were hurt and jealous; brothers got rid of him; brothers lied to their father.*

2. "What did we say were the four reasons Joseph's half brothers hated him?"

> • *They were hurt and jealous from their father's showing favoritism toward Joseph. (The "coat of many colors" was a sign of being special. People who wore such coats did not work in the fields because the coats were long and would get caught in the bushes. Thus, Joseph seemed not to have to do the same kind of hard field work as his brothers.)*

> • *Because Joseph told their father a bad report about them. This rubbed them the wrong way, even if they were wrong.*

> *Here they were working hard, and Joseph told on them.*

> • *Because Joseph had dreams that made him seem above them*

> • *Because Joseph was insensitive to his brothers' feelings and kept telling them his dreams, even though they didn't like it; Joseph didn't seem to even notice that they hated him.*

ASK:

3. "What were Joseph's character weaknesses?"

> • *Insensitivity to others' feelings, poor relationship skills.*

> • *Pride, haughtiness, arrogance. His reports of his dreams were full of pride. There was no sense of why he had risen to a high position in his dreams (such as helping other people). His focus was only on his family's bowing down to him.*

ASK:

4. "How did his family's problems contribute to these weaknesses? How did he learn to be this way in his family?"

> • *From being treated extra special and different, Joseph learned to feel that he was special, above his brothers, not having to worry about what they felt. Also, he probably did not feel like "one of the boys" and so never developed a close relationship with them. Sometimes when people feel like outsiders, they don't know how to build close, caring relationships. They keep alienating other people, which then just makes them more of an outsider, in turn leading them to stop trying.*

5. "What do you think the story is suggesting is the purpose for Joseph's being thrown out of his family and sold into slavery in Egypt? What does the story sug-

gest about what family problems can lead to?"

> • *Joseph had to deal with his character weaknesses if he was ever going to be a great man. He had visions of greatness, but he did not have the character that could make him great. He might very well have become a tyrant, so insensitive was he.*

> • *This is what the men in the video "Glory" experienced. The challenges, fears, and struggles they faced forced them to grow up and become true heroes. Family problems don't have to destroy you. They can be your call to grow into true manhood. But you have to seize the opportunity. You have to heed the call. That is the message of this part of the story.*

BREAK
(15 minutes for groups)

EXERCISE: IDENTIFYING YOUR CHARACTER GROWTH GOALS

The character areas the boys will examine are the same ones in the Oath of Manhood. It is your opportunity to teach them more fully the meaning of the various character traits of manhood. You will have to draw deeply on your own beliefs about these traits and your own experiences as a man to help the boys understand their meaning.

FATHERS:
This is an opportunity to teach your values to your son. Help him understand what these traits of manhood mean to you and why they are important.

GROUP LEADERS:
For each of the traits below, ask different men to give examples from their own lives of how they have lived out – or failed to live out – these traits. The goal is for the boys to see specifically how important these traits are that they recite each week and what they actually look like in men's lives. For each trait:

> 1. RECITE: Recite with the boys the Oath dealing with that trait.
> 2. ASK: Ask them what they think it means.
> 3. EXPLAIN: Tell them what it means to you. Give them a few examples out of your own life if possible.
> 4. BRAINSTORM: Have your boys come up with examples of how they can demonstrate that trait in their own lives. Help them if they can't think of any.
> 5. EVALUATE: Have the boys rate themselves on the Character Growth Chart in their workbook.
> 6. SHARE: Have the boys share their ratings and why they rated themselves that way.
> 7. COMMIT: Ask each boy who rates himself low on a trait if he is willing to commit to growing in that area.

PRAY:
This time should be a solemn one in which the commitments the boys made to grow in their low areas are placed before the Lord.

> 1. REVIEW: Have each boy stand and name the three character traits

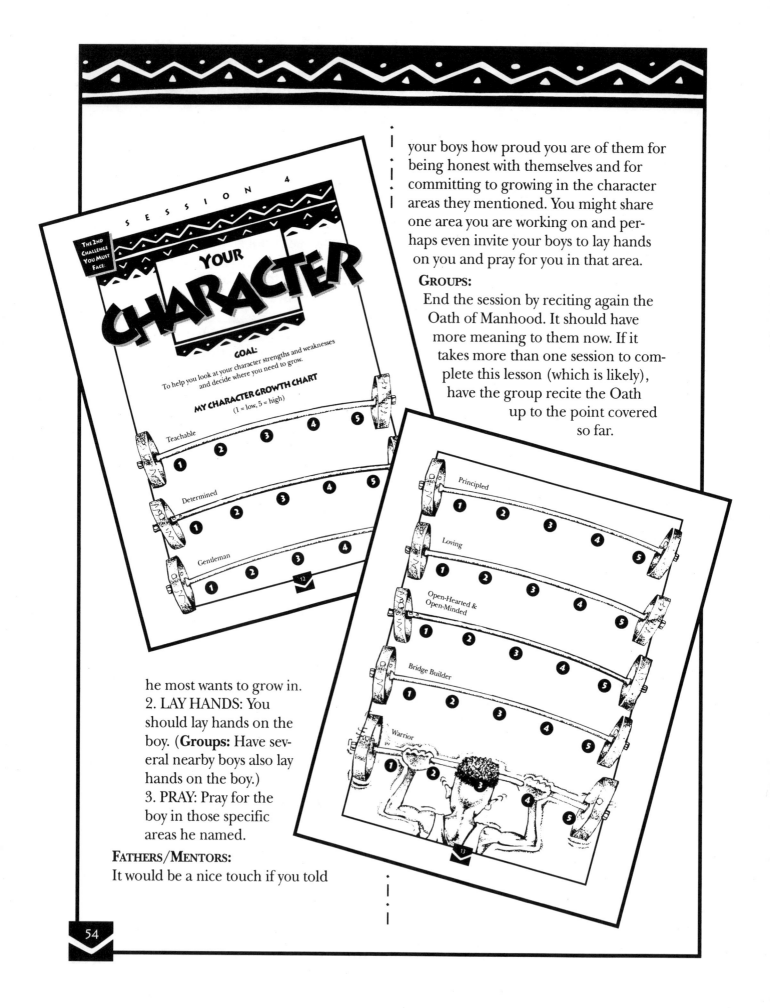

your boys how proud you are of them for being honest with themselves and for committing to growing in the character areas they mentioned. You might share one area you are working on and perhaps even invite your boys to lay hands on you and pray for you in that area.

GROUPS:

End the session by reciting again the Oath of Manhood. It should have more meaning to them now. If it takes more than one session to complete this lesson (which is likely), have the group recite the Oath up to the point covered so far.

SESSION 4

THE 2ND CHALLENGE YOU MUST FACE:

YOUR CHARACTER

GOAL:

To help you look at your character strengths and weaknesses and decide where you need to grow.

MY CHARACTER GROWTH CHART

(1 = low, 5 = high)

	1	2	3	4	5
Teachable	1	2	3	4	5
Determined	1	2	3	4	5
Gentleman	1	2	3	4	

12

	1	2	3	4	5
Principled	1	2	3	4	5
Loving	1	2	3	4	5
Open-Hearted & Open-Minded	1	2	3	4	5
Bridge Builder	1	2	3	4	5
Warrior	1	2	3	4	5

13

---

he most wants to grow in.

2. LAY HANDS: You should lay hands on the boy. (**Groups:** Have several nearby boys also lay hands on the boy.)

3. PRAY: Pray for the boy in those specific areas he named.

FATHERS/MENTORS:

It would be a nice touch if you told

THIRD CHALLENGE—BOYS IN THE 'HOOD

This session helps boys look at the challenge of peer pressure, especially from other boys.

GOALS

At the end of this session, boys will be able to:

1. Understand the meaning and importance of sowing and reaping (consequences).
2. Understand the concept of peer pressure.
3. Identify the qualities of a good friend.
4. Commit to picking good friends.

MATERIALS NEEDED

• This manual • Student workbooks
• Bibles • The Oath of Manhood • The Road to Manhood map • A pack of plant seeds

WARM UP

1. Have your boys recite the Oath of Manhood. You may end in a prayer for learning and growth or a moment of quiet meditation on what they want to get out of this session. **FATHERS/MENTORS:** Recite the Oath with your boys.

VILLAGE TALK

2. Village Talk: This time is to provide boys with an opportunity to talk about the ways they have experienced various aspects of their manhood training since the last meeting.

OPENING ACTIVITY: SOWING AND REAPING

HAND OUT:
Give each boy a seed. Don't let the packet be seen by the boys.

ASK:
1. "What happens when you put this seed in the ground?"
   • *It starts to grow.*
2. "Can you see it growing?"
   • *Not at first, but eventually you do.*
3. "Does anyone know what kind of plant this seed is?"
   • *No, you can't tell.*
4. "When will you know?"
   • *After it grows and you can see what kind of plant or fruit it produces.*

READ:
Have a boy read Galatians 6:7-9.

ASK:
1. "What does 'sow' mean?"
   - *Explain what "sow" means.*
2. "What does 'reap' mean?"
   - *Explain what "reap" means.*
3. "What does Paul mean when he says, 'A man reaps what he sows'?"
   - *It means that wherever you put a seed in the ground, the plant that comes up is already determined. If you plant an apple tree seed, an apple tree is going to grow. If you plant a tomato plant seed, a tomato plant is going to grow.*
4. "If I plant a strawberry seed, is a blueberry bush going to grow?"
   - *No.*
5. "So Paul is saying in verse 8 that if you start giving your sinful nature soil to grow in – if you plant it, water it, and fertilize it – what are you going to reap?"
   - *Destruction.*

SAY:
Give examples of sowing to the sinful nature and reaping destruction.

BRAINSTORM:
Ask your boys what other examples they can think of.

ASK:
"When Paul says in verse 8 that if you sow to please the Spirit, you will reap eternal life, what does he mean?"
   - *Explain.*

SAY:
"Now let's look at some boys who sowed seeds of destruction."

READ:
Have the boys take turns reading Genesis 37:2-28.

ASK:
"What kind of boys were Joseph's brothers? What bad seeds did they plant?"
   - *The seed of Disobedience. Joseph had to bring a bad report about them when they were supposed to be tending the flocks.*
   - *They also planted the seeds of Jealousy and Hatred, storing them up in their hearts.*
"What fruit did those seeds produce?"
   - *Destruction of their relationship with Joseph. They threw him into the pit and then sold him into slavery. That's how much they hated Joseph.*

BREAK
(15 minutes for groups)

EXERCISE:
THE FRUIT TREE

Have the boys turn in their workbooks to "The Tree of Bad Fruit."

READ:
Ask a boy to read Matthew 7:15-20. Explain the passage to the boys.

SAY:
"Jesus says that some people pretend to be good. They pretend to be our friends, but they are not. How can you tell if someone is truly a good person for you to be around?"
   - *Looking at their fruit – the things they do and say.*

things in the picture of the Tree of Bad Fruit.

ASK:

"What good fruit do some boys produce? What good fruit should you be on the lookout for in your friends?"

BRAINSTORM:

Have them think about the boys they know who do good things. Have them fill in some of those things in the picture of the Tree of Good Fruit.

SESSION 5

THE 3RD CHALLENGE YOU MUST FACE:

YOUR FRIENDS

GOAL:

To help you look at your friends so that you choose friends who will help you be good and accomplish your goals.

THE TREE OF BAD FRUIT

The Fruit Tree

14

THE TREE OF GOOD FRUIT

The Fruit Tree

MY FRUITY FRIENDS

Friend: _____

Good Fruit

_____   Bad Fruit

Friend: _____

Good Fruit

_____   Bad Fruit

15

"So we have to learn to look at the fruit in our friends' lives."

ASK:

"What bad fruit do some boys produce? What bad fruit should you be on the look-out for in your friends?"

BRAINSTORM:

Have them think about boys they know who do bad things. Have them fill in some of those

REFLECT:

Point out the Oath of Manhood to them. Tell them that the Oath is filled with good seeds. If they plant those seeds – those attitudes – in their lives, they will produce excellent fruit.

APPLY:

Have the boys turn in their workbooks to "My Fruity Friends."

Tell them to pick two of their friends. Have them list the good and bad fruit they see in those persons' lives.

COMMIT:

Have your boys commit to themselves, to you, and to God that they will watch out for bad fruit people.

NOTES

_____

_____

_____

_____

_____

_____

_____

_____

_____

_____

_____

_____

_____

FOURTH CHALLENGE— OPPRESSION OF BLACK MEN

This session helps boys to identify the various ways in which American society oppresses African American men.

GOALS

At the end of this session, boys will be able to:
1. Understand the concepts of oppression and racism.
2. Understand the variety of obstacles black men face in American society.
3. Understand the importance of trying "twice as hard" and being "twice as good."
4. Affirm their value to God.

MATERIALS NEEDED

• This manual • Student workbooks • Bibles • The Oath of Manhood • The Road to Manhood map

WARM UP

1. Have your boys recite the Oath of Manhood. You may end in a prayer for learning and growth or a moment of quiet meditation on what they want to get out of this session. **FATHERS/MENTORS:** Recite the Oath with your boys.

VILLAGE TALK

2. Village Talk: This time is to provide boys with an opportunity to talk about the ways they have experienced various aspects of their manhood training since the last meeting.

OPENING ACTIVITY: REAL LIFE STORIES

ELDER TALE 1:
Tell the boys a story from your own life concerning discrimination you have experienced. Help them to understand that discrimination is still real and alive.

ELDER TALE 2:
There are two times in this curriculum when we ask you to expose your boys to other men. This is one of those times. Your goal is to ask at least two other men to share their stories of trying to make it as black men in this society. Either have the men come to you and your boys, or you go to the men. This will be a power-

ful time of learning for your boys, because these will be real life stories.

Ask the men to share on these topics:

- What did you face? What was the situation?
- How did it make you feel?
- How did you handle it? Did you get any help?
- What lessons did you learn from it?

One lesson black people have always taught their children in the face of American racism is the importance of trying twice as hard and being twice as good as their white counterparts in order to keep even. You should emphasize this to your boys.

READ:
Have a boy read Psalm 139:1-5, 14.

EXPLAIN:
Explain the text to them. Talk to them about their value to God and how God made them with great value. Emphasize that no matter how other people may treat them, they have great value to God, for they were created in God's image.

AFFIRMATION:
Have the boys turn in their workbooks to "God's View of Me." Have them fill out the affirmation based on Psalm 139.

PRAYER:
Have your boys thank God for making them beautiful.

COMMITTING TO YOUR DREAMS

This session helps boys realize that they must pursue the valuable dreams God has placed in their hearts, even when it costs them.

GOALS

At the end of this session, your boys will be able to:

1. Understand the importance of dreams.
2. Identify their own dreams for their lives.
3. Turn their dreams into achievable goals for this year.
4. Commit to achieving their goals.

MATERIALS NEEDED

• This manual • Student workbooks
• Bibles • The Oath of Manhood • The Road to Manhood map

WARM UP

1. Have your boys recite the Oath of Manhood. You may end in a prayer for learning and growth or a moment of quiet meditation on what they want to get out of this session. **FATHERS/MENTORS:** Recite the Oath with your boys.

VILLAGE TALK

2. Village Talk: This time is to provide boys with an opportunity to talk about the ways they have experienced various aspects of their manhood training since the last meeting.

OPENING ACTIVITY: WHAT ARE YOU LOOKING FOR?

ASK:

Ask the following questions, and encourage discussion:

1. "What would make your life truly special and fulfilling if you could have it?"

2. "What right now is the most important person or thing in your life?"

3. "As you think about your future, what do you think is most critical to making sure you have a great life?"

> • *Be sure to thank each boy for his contribution, but don't give away any bias of your own right now. Try to discover what is most important to these boys.*

This is basically a warm-up activity to get the boys thinking about this topic.

READ:

Have the boys take turns reading Genesis 37:3-11.

ASK:

1. "What were Joseph's dreams for his life?"

> • *That one day he would be great and that his family would bow down to him.*

2. "What reaction did his brothers have to his dreams?"

> • *They hated him for having the dreams and hated him also for telling them the dreams (Genesis 37:8).*

3. "Did Joseph's dreams come true? Did his family one day bow down to him?"

> • *Yes, over 22 years later.*

4. "What can we learn from the fact that before Joseph's dreams came true, he was betrayed by his brothers, sold into slavery, lied about, and thrown into prison for many years?"

> • *That dreams take time, but if God puts the dream in our hearts, we can overcome any obstacle.*

ELDER TALE:

Tell your boys about a dream you had that took a long time to come true. Say what you had to learn and do before the dream could become a reality. Then emphasize that to become a true man we have to find our dreams and follow them.

EXPLORATION: MY DREAMS FOR ME

Have your boys turn to their workbooks and fill out the "My Dreams for Me" form. They will probably need help in some sections. It is important to understand that many African American boys do not have dreams for their lives. You may have to coach them to think about what they want to be different in their lives and what they want in the long run.

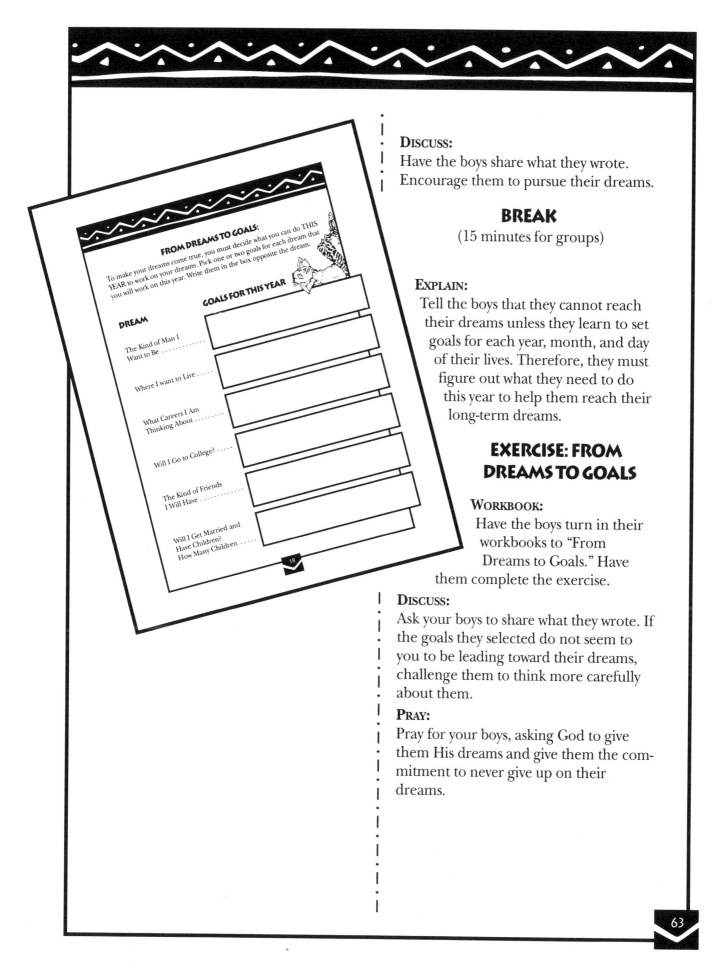

FROM DREAMS TO GOALS:

To make your dreams come true, you must decide what you can do THIS YEAR to work on your dreams. Pick one or two goals for each dream that you will work on this year. Write them in the box opposite the dream.

DREAM

GOALS FOR THIS YEAR

The Kind of Man I Want to Be . . . .

Where I want to Live . . . . . .

What Careers I Am Thinking About . . . .

Will I Go to College? . . . . .

The Kind of Friends I Will Have . . . .

Will I Get Married and Have Children? How Many Children . . . . .

18

DISCUSS:

Have the boys share what they wrote. Encourage them to pursue their dreams.

BREAK

(15 minutes for groups)

EXPLAIN:

Tell the boys that they cannot reach their dreams unless they learn to set goals for each year, month, and day of their lives. Therefore, they must figure out what they need to do this year to help them reach their long-term dreams.

EXERCISE: FROM DREAMS TO GOALS

WORKBOOK:

Have the boys turn in their workbooks to "From Dreams to Goals." Have them complete the exercise.

DISCUSS:

Ask your boys to share what they wrote. If the goals they selected do not seem to you to be leading toward their dreams, challenge them to think more carefully about them.

PRAY:

Pray for your boys, asking God to give them His dreams and give them the commitment to never give up on their dreams.

NOTES

UPS AND DOWNS OF THE HERO'S JOURNEY

This session reinforces the concept that the hero's journey, although ultimately victorious, is full of ups and downs.

GOALS

At the end of this session, boys will be able to:

1. Understand the concept of "life journey."
2. Understand that every man on his journey to manhood has ups and downs.
3. Affirm that God is with us in all our ups and downs, shaping us into His image.

MATERIALS NEEDED

• This manual • Student workbooks • Bibles • The Oath of Manhood • The Road to Manhood map • Newsprint or chalkboard

WARM UP

1. Have your boys recite the Oath of Manhood. You may end in a prayer for learning and growth or a moment of quiet meditation on what they want to get out of this session. **FATHERS/MENTORS:** Recite the Oath with your boys. ·

VILLAGE TALK

2. Village Talk: This time is to provide boys with an opportunity to talk about the ways they have experienced various aspects of their manhood training since the last meeting.

OPENING ACTIVITY: LIFE MAP

ELDER TALE:

Before this session, draw on newsprint a timeline of some of the key ups and downs in your life, with a focus on the events which helped or hindered your achievement of your goals as a boy/man. You must use your discretion about what to put down, of course, but try to give your boys some sense of your life journey.

SESSION 8

UPS & DOWNS OF YOUR HERO'S JOURNEY

GOAL:

To help you understand that every man's life has its ups and downs. Heroes are men who don't give up, but finish the journey. They know God is always with them.

MY JOURNEY SO FAR
In the space below, draw a timeline of your life so far. Be sure to show the ups and downs. Think about: • Relationships you have had (family, friends) • School • Sports • Successes • Failures • Places you have gone • Feelings you have had

---

REFLECTION:
Now have your boys turn to "My Journey So Far" in their workbooks and draw a timeline of their life so far. Ask them to think about:

- Relationships they've had (family, friends)
- School
- Sports
- Successes, failures
- Places they have gone
- Feelings they have had

SHARING:
Have the boys share their timelines. Ask them why they described an event as an up or a down.

READING:
Have the boys take turns reading Genesis 39 (entire chapter).

DISCUSSION:
Go over with the boys the ups and downs Joseph experienced.

- *Ups: Rose to number two position in Potiphar's house; resisted the temptations of Potiphar's wife; rose to number two position in prison.*

- *Downs: Sold to Potiphar as a slave; lied about by Potiphar's wife; thrown into prison.*

AFFIRMATION:
Point out to the boys the repeated phrase, "But the Lord was with Joseph." Emphasize that in all our ups and downs, God will be with us. Point out on the Road to Manhood Map how there are many ups and downs.

READING:
Have a boy read Job 23:10. Explain the concept of God's using our downs to shape us.

PRAYER:
Have the boys thank God that he is using the ups and downs to make us like gold, shaping our character.

AVOIDING THE FALSE MANHOOD TRAP

This session exposes boys to the perils along the way to manhood and helps them identify ways in which they may currently be "at risk."

GOALS

At the end of this session, boys will be able to:
1. Understand the concept of "false manhood."
2. Identify a variety of paths that men take which lead to false manhood.
3. Assess their own risk status.

MATERIALS NEEDED

• This manual • Student workbooks
• Bibles • The Oath of Manhood • The Road to Manhood map

WARM UP

1. Have your boys recite the Oath of Manhood. You may end in a prayer for learning and growth or a moment of quiet meditation on what they want to get out of this session. **FATHERS/MENTORS:** Recite the Oath with your boys.

VILLAGE TALK

2. Village Talk: This time is to provide boys with an opportunity to talk about the ways they have experienced various aspects of their manhood training since the last meeting.

OPENING ACTIVITY: TRUE OR FALSE

READ:
Have a boy read Matthew 7:13-14. Explain what Jesus is talking about.

EXPLAIN:
As you point to the large Road to Manhood Map which you have drawn on newsprint, show the boys the various paths that lead boys off the road to true manhood down into the Swamp of False Manhood. Note the many pitfalls (the dark circles) in the swamp. Point out that the road to Authentic Manhood gets narrower and narrower (as Jesus said) and curves all around. It requires making constant choices to stay on track because

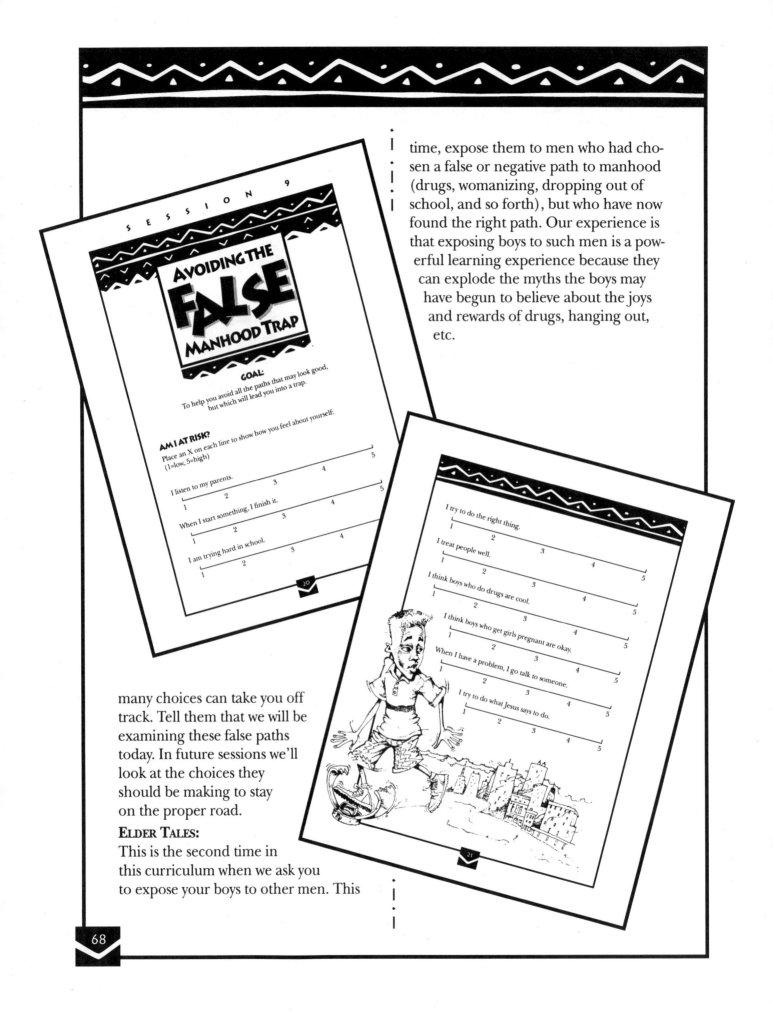

time, expose them to men who had chosen a false or negative path to manhood (drugs, womanizing, dropping out of school, and so forth), but who have now found the right path. Our experience is that exposing boys to such men is a powerful learning experience because they can explode the myths the boys may have begun to believe about the joys and rewards of drugs, hanging out, etc.

SESSION 9

AVOIDING THE FALSE MANHOOD TRAP

GOAL:
To help you avoid all the paths that may look good, but which will lead you into a trap.

AM I AT RISK?
Place an X on each line to show how you feel about yourself:
(1=low, 5=high)

I listen to my parents.
1 — 2 — 3 — 4 — 5

When I start something, I finish it.
1 — 2 — 3 — 4 — 5

I am trying hard in school.
1 — 2 — 3 — 4 — 5

20

I try to do the right thing.
1 — 2 — 3 — 4 — 5

I treat people well.
1 — 2 — 3 — 4 — 5

I think boys who do drugs are cool.
1 — 2 — 3 — 4 — 5

I think boys who get girls pregnant are okay.
1 — 2 — 3 — 4 — 5

When I have a problem, I go talk to someone.
1 — 2 — 3 — 4 — 5

I try to do what Jesus says to do.
1 — 2 — 3 — 4 — 5

21

---

many choices can take you off track. Tell them that we will be examining these false paths today. In future sessions we'll look at the choices they should be making to stay on the proper road.

ELDER TALES:

This is the second time in this curriculum when we ask you to expose your boys to other men. This

After each man tells his story, ask your boys what they heard about what leads a man off the road to authentic manhood.

- What lies did the speaker believe?
- What rewards or pleasure did he think he was going to get?
- What brought him to his senses?

REFLECT:

Now have your boys turn in their workbooks to "Am I At Risk?" to assess their own risk status. The "risk factors" listed are ones that boys who get into trouble when they get older often start showing when they are younger. You will probably have to help them get started in putting an X at the appropriate place on the scale.

SHARE:

Have the boys share their answers. Discuss with them what they mean by each answer and why they put the X where they did.

COMMIT:

Have the boys express to God their commitment to stay on the true road to manhood. Have them ask God to give them wisdom to stay off the false trails.

NOTES

_____

_____

_____

_____

_____

_____

_____

_____

_____

_____

_____

CHOICES AUTHENTIC MEN KEEP MAKING

CHOICE 1—CHOOSE TO EXCEL, NO MATTER WHAT

This session encourages the boys never to give up trying to be the best they can be, no matter what obstacles they encounter.

GOALS

At the end of this session, your boys will be able to:
1. Identify what inner attitudes cause some people to give up.
2. Identify what inner attitudes cause other people to get up when life knocks them down.

MATERIALS NEEDED

• This manual • Student workbooks
• Bibles • The Oath of Manhood • The Road to Manhood map • Videocassette player • Video: *Chariots of Fire* (or appropriate video about not giving up in the face of difficulty)

WARM UP

1. Have your boys recite the Oath of Manhood. You may end in a prayer for learning and growth or a moment of quiet meditation on what they want to get out of this session. **FATHERS/MENTORS:** Recite the Oath with your boys.

VILLAGE TALK

2.
Village Talk: This time is to provide boys with an opportunity to talk about the ways they have experienced various aspects of their manhood training since the last meeting.

OPENING ACTIVITY

READ:
Have the boys take turns reading Genesis 39:1-23.

ASK:
1. "What happened to Joseph in this part of the story?"

> • *He rose to a great position in Potiphar's house, then was unfairly accused of attempted rape by Potiphar's wife. He was thrown into prison, where he began to rise again to an important position.*

2. "Do you think Joseph was tempted to give up after he had gone to such trouble to do well with the tasks he was given in Potiphar's house, only to be thrown into

prison on trumped-up charges?"

> • *Yes, everyone would be tempted to give up.*

3. "Why do you think Joseph didn't give up either when he was first sold into slavery to Potiphar or when he was thrown into prison? What made him continue to try to excel?"

> • *His faith in the Lord, his commitment to excellence, his faith in himself.*

EXPLORE:

Select a video dealing with someone facing obstacles and challenges, but not giving up. While *Chariots of Fire* is a good one (its major drawback is that it is not about black people), many other videos will do as well, such as *Stand and Deliver, The Dead Poets Society, Heart of Stone,* etc.

SAY:

"Today we are going to watch a video about someone who faced challenges as great as Joseph did."

SHOW:

Chariots of Fire video (or similar video).

ASK:

1. "What challenges did the people in the video face?" (In the case of *Chariots of Fire,* focus on Eric Liddel.)

2. "Do you think they were tempted to give up?"

3. "What did they have to do to overcome these obstacles?"

> • *In the case of* Chariots of Fire, *years of hard work; coaching by someone who knew how to win; willingness to try again after a failure; smaller events leading up to the big event.*

SAY:

"We will end our session today right here. Next time we are going to pick this session up and talk about its implications for our own lives."

CHOICES AUTHENTIC MEN KEEP MAKING

CHOOSE TO EXCEL, NO MATTER WHAT (CONT.)

This session continues to encourage the boys never to give up trying to be the best they can be, no matter what obstacles they encounter.

GOALS

At the end of this session, your boys will be able to:
1. Identify what rewards there are for giving up.
2. Identify the rewards for choosing to excel.
3. Identify the challenges in their own lives.
4. Commit to excelling.
5. Recite a Scripture verse affirming the importance of not giving up.

MATERIALS NEEDED

• This manual • Student workbooks • Bibles • The Oath of Manhood • The Road to Manhood map

WARM UP

1. Have your boys recite the Oath of Manhood. You may end in a prayer for learning and growth or a moment of quiet meditation on what they want to get out of this session. **FATHERS/MENTORS:** Recite the Oath with your boys.

VILLAGE TALK

2. Village Talk: This time is to provide boys with an opportunity to talk about the ways they have experienced various aspects of their manhood training since the last meeting.

OPENING ACTIVITY: HIDDEN PAYOFFS OF TRYING VS. GIVING UP

WORKBOOK:
Have your boys turn in their workbooks to "Hidden Payoffs."

BRAINSTORM:
Discuss possible payoffs for each character described. Most are boys who have given up trying to do well.

ASK:
(Regarding the characters in "Hidden Payoffs") "Who got the best rewards?"
   • *The Class Star*
Point out that while you may get something from giving up and acting bad, the most positive payoffs come from doing well.

CHOICE 1: CHOOSE TO EXCEL NO MATTER WHAT

GOAL:

To teach you to never give up, but to go for the reward of always doing your best, no matter what happens.

HIDDEN PAYOFFS

THE SECRET REWARDS OF SUCCESS AND FAILURE

Everyone gets a reward for what they do, even if what they do can be considered a failure. "You reap what you sow." You get paid for what you do. Sometimes the payoffs are out in the open, obvious. But sometimes the payoffs are hidden from the view of other people and often from the view of the person who is getting paid. The way to discover a hidden payoff is to ask, "What's in it for me (or him)? What am I (is he) getting out of this?"

Can you discover the hidden payoffs the following people get?

THE CLASS CLOWN

Jerry loved fun. He loved to enjoy life. So far so good. But Jerry never stopped trying to have fun. He was always fooling around, cracking jokes, and generally causing a little mischief – even in class. No matter how hard they tried, Jerry's teachers could not

22

COMMITMENT:

1. READ Philippians 3:12-14.

2. EXPLAIN what Paul's attitude was toward giving up.

3. MEMORIZE: Have your boys memorize this part of the passage: ". . . One thing I do: Forgetting what is behind and straining toward what is ahead, I press on toward the goal to win the prize for which God has called me . . ." (Philippians 3:13-14).

---

stop him from clowning around. What were Jerry's payoffs?

_____

_____

THE BULLY

"Roger the Terrible" was big, strong, and mean. If you crossed him – and often even if you didn't – you were going to pay big time. You'd be lucky if he just roughed you up a little and "taxed" you some of your lunch money. People didn't mess with Roger. Of course, Roger didn't have any true friends, either. What were his payoffs?

_____

_____

THE CLASS STAR

Malcom was an excellent student. He always did well on tests, knew the answers when the teacher called on him, and generally seemed to enjoy school. He even helped other students out. What were his payoffs?

_____

_____

THE DROPOUT

Keith started out when he was young enjoying school. He had always been anxious to get to school and see his friends. Many times, the lessons in class were interesting, although he hadn't done very well, even when

23

DISCUSS:

Ask your boys to identify which of the payoffs discussed so far they have gotten by their own behaviors. Try to communicate that while it is understandable why some people would rather give up, we will ultimately be happier if we don't give up but keep trying.

First, have them read it ten times. Then have them close the Bible and recite it three times from memory. **GROUP LEADERS:** Go around the room and have each boy recite it aloud.

4. ENCOURAGE them to memorize the entire passage (vv. 12-14). Tell them that they will have to remember these verses in the future, and to keep practicing them.

5. ENCOURAGE them to endure, to persevere, to press on toward the prize for which God has called them.

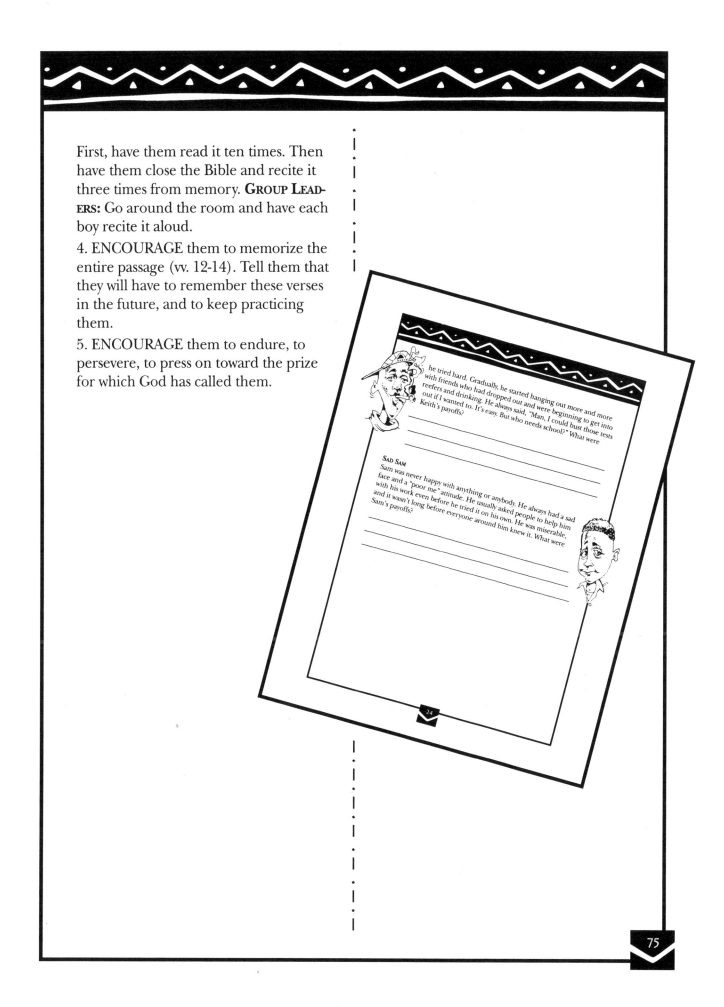

he tried hard. Gradually, he started hanging out more and more with friends who had dropped out and were beginning to get into reefers and drinking. He always said, "Man, I could bust those tests out if I wanted to. It's easy. But who needs school?" What were Keith's payoffs?

_____

_____

SAD SAM

Sam was never happy with anything or anybody. He always had a sad face and a "poor me" attitude. He usually asked people to help him with his work even before he tried it on his own. He was miserable, and it wasn't long before everyone around him knew it. What were Sam's payoffs?

_____

_____

_____

24

CHOICES AUTHENTIC MEN KEEP MAKING

CHOICE 2 — CHOOSE INTEGRITY

This session encourages boys to make decisions based on values rooted in biblical principles. It teaches the critical questions they must answer before they do things.

GOALS

At the end of this session, your boys will be able to:
1. Identify situations calling for moral decisions.
2. Identify biblical reasons for making moral decisions.
3. Work out the moral decisions for situations they currently face or are likely to face.

MATERIALS NEEDED

• This manual • Student workbooks • Bibles • The Oath of Manhood • Road to Manhood map • Newsprint or chalkboard

WARM UP

1. Have your boys recite the Oath of Manhood. You may end in a prayer for learning and growth or in a moment of quiet meditation on what they want to get out of this session. **FATHERS/MENTORS:** Recite the Oath with your boys.

VILLAGE TALK

2. Village Talk: This time is to provide boys with an opportunity to talk about the ways they have experienced various aspects of their manhood training since the last meeting.

OPENING ACTIVITY

READ:
Have the boys take turns reading Genesis 39:1-23.

ASK:
1. "What kind of man was Joseph physically?"
   • *Well built and handsome.*
2. "What did Potiphar's wife do?"
   • *She attempted to seduce him into a sexual affair with her.*
3. "Do you think she was used to men turning her down?"
   • *Probably not.*
4. "What kind of woman do you think she was?"
   • *Willing to be unfaithful to her husband; willing to lie and accuse falsely;*

selfish; used to power and getting her own way; maybe used to intimidating the slaves and servants.

5. "Let's look at the three stages of what happened between Joseph and Mrs. Potiphar so that we can see how Joseph reacted to her."

FATHERS/MENTORS:

Have your boys turn in their workbooks to "Stages of a Bad Relationship." Have the boys fill in the answers as you go along.

FOR GROUPS:

Write each stage on a sheet of newsprint so that the boys can all see it. Have them turn in their workbooks to "Stages of a Bad Relationship" and fill in the answers as you write them on the newsprint. Get them to answer the questions as much as possible before you give them the answers. Set up the newsprint as follows:

STAGES OF A BAD RELATIONSHIP

STAGE 1:
Mrs. Potiphar: "Come to bed with me."
Joseph's Response (Genesis 39:8-9):
    1.
    2.
        A.
        B.
        C.

STAGE 2:
Mrs. Potiphar: Kept at him "day after day."
Joseph's Response (Genesis 39:10):
    1.
    2.

STAGE 3:
Mrs. Potiphar: Got him alone and grabbed him.
Joseph's Response (Genesis 39:11-12):
    1.

STAGE 4:
Mrs. Potiphar: False accusation of rape.
Potiphar's Response: Believed his wife. Sent Joseph to prison.
Joseph's Response:

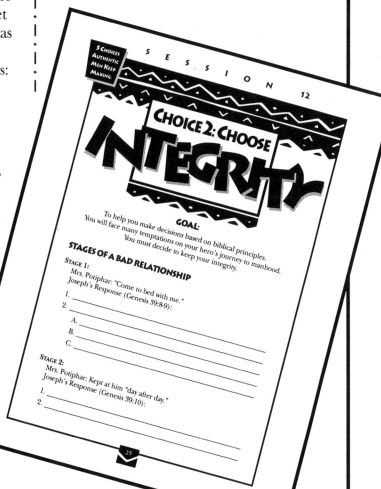

5 CHOICES AUTHENTIC MEN KEEP MAKING.

S E S S I O N 12

CHOICE 2: CHOOSE INTEGRITY

GOAL:
To help you make decisions based on biblical principles. You will face many temptations on your hero's journey to manhood. You must decide to keep your integrity.

STAGES OF A BAD RELATIONSHIP

STAGE 1:
Mrs. Potiphar: "Come to bed with me."
Joseph's Response (Genesis 39:8-9):
1. _____
2. _____
   A. _____
   B. _____
   C. _____

STAGE 2:
Mrs. Potiphar: Kept at him "day after day."
Joseph's Response (Genesis 39:10):
1. _____
2. _____

25

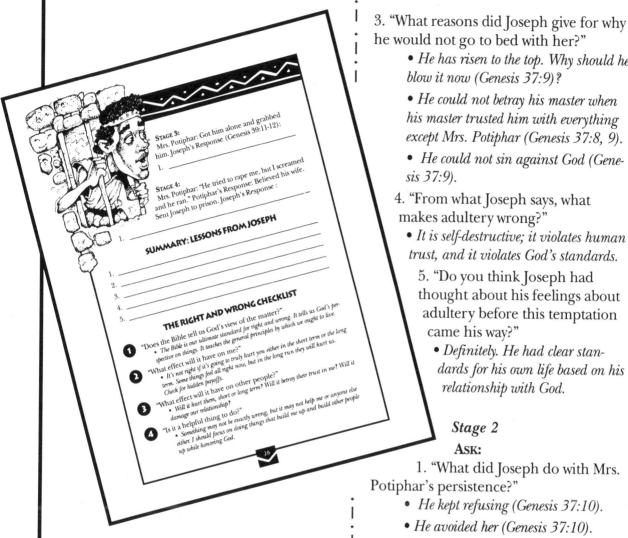

STAGE 3:
Mrs. Potiphar: Got him alone and grabbed him. Joseph's Response (Genesis 39:11-12):

1. _____

STAGE 4:
Mrs. Potiphar: "He tried to rape me, but I screamed and he ran." Potiphar's Response: Believed his wife. Sent Joseph to prison. Joseph's Response :

1. _____

SUMMARY: LESSONS FROM JOSEPH

1. _____
2. _____
3. _____
4. _____
5. _____

THE RIGHT AND WRONG CHECKLIST

1 "Does the Bible tell us God's view of the matter?"
• The Bible is our ultimate standard for right and wrong. It tells us God's perspective on things. It teaches the general principles by which we ought to live.

2 "What effect will it have on me?"
• It's not right if it's going to truly hurt you either in the short term or the long term. Some things feel all right now, but in the long run they will hurt us. Check for hidden payoffs.

3 "What effect will it have on other people?"
• Will it hurt them, short or long term? Will it betray their trust in me? Will it damage our relationship?

4 "Is it a helpful thing to do?"
• Something may not be exactly wrong, but it may not help me or anyone else either. I should focus on doing things that build me up and build other people up while honoring God.

26

---

3. "What reasons did Joseph give for why he would not go to bed with her?"

• *He has risen to the top. Why should he blow it now (Genesis 37:9)?*

• *He could not betray his master when his master trusted him with everything except Mrs. Potiphar (Genesis 37:8, 9).*

• *He could not sin against God (Genesis 37:9).*

4. "From what Joseph says, what makes adultery wrong?"

• *It is self-destructive; it violates human trust, and it violates God's standards.*

5. "Do you think Joseph had thought about his feelings about adultery before this temptation came his way?"

• *Definitely. He had clear standards for his own life based on his relationship with God.*

Stage 2
ASK:

1. "What did Joseph do with Mrs. Potiphar's persistence?"

• *He kept refusing (Genesis 37:10).*

• *He avoided her (Genesis 37:10).*

2. "Why does Joseph now avoid Mrs. Potiphar?"

• *Because she won't take "no" for an answer.*

Stage 3

ASK:

"What does Joseph do when Mrs. Potiphar corners and grabs him?"

• *Runs out of the house (Genesis 37:12).*

Stage 4

ASK:

"What four things does Joseph do when

Stage 1

ASK:

1. "When Mrs. Potiphar approached Joseph, do you think he was tempted to have sex with her?"

• *Probably, since he was a healthy male with normal drives.*

2. "What did Joseph do with this temptation at this stage?"

• *He refused (Genesis 37:8).*

• *He tried to reason with her.*

the temptation to have an affair comes from Mrs. Potiphar?"

• *Refuses to give in.*
• *Tries to reason with the person.*
• *When the person won't listen, he avoids her.*
• *In a hot moment of extreme difficulty, he runs from her.*

SUMMARY:

"What can I learn from Joseph about maintaining my integrity?" (List these on the newsprint so your boys can see them while they fill in the answers in their workbooks.)

1. Think before I act. (Think through my personal standards before I get into a situation.)

2. Just say no. (Refuse to give in.)

3. Know what I believe and say it. Have solid reasons for why I shouldn't do something bad or why I should do something good. Be able to share those reasons with people who may be tempting me. If it is my own inner voice tempting me, I need to reason with myself.

4. Avoid trouble. (When reasoning doesn't work, then I should avoid any situations which might tempt me.)

5. If all else fails, run. (When I get in a tight situation and am seriously tempted, I should run, get out, and don't come back.)

BREAK
(15 minutes for groups)

EXPLORATION: TEMPTATIONS BOYS FACE

ASK:
"What temptations do boys your age often face?"

WRITE:
Record on newsprint the answers boys give. You will need this list shortly.

BRAINSTORM:
Explore whatever answers your boys give.

DISCUSS:
Discuss briefly the temptations they bring up.

EXERCISE: HOW TO MAKE MORAL DECISIONS

ASK:
"When facing temptation, we have to make a moral decision. How can we know when the decisions we are making are right?"

BRAINSTORM:
Let boys give several answers.

WORKBOOK:
Have your boys turn to "The Right and Wrong Checklist."

DISCUSS:
Go through the checklist (see page 79) and explain each concept, using Joseph as an example.

EXERCISE: YOU BE THE JUDGE
(For Groups)

SAY:
"Let's play a game."

A. DIVIDE THE GROUP:

Divide the group into two teams. Appoint three boys to be judges. Tell them that God has appointed them to be His representatives with this group of boys. They are to decide which team has made the right decision, and which team has the best reasons and strategy for their decision. So they are to judge:

1. The Decision: Is it right or wrong?

2. The Reasons: Which group's reasons make the most sense?

3. The Strategy: Which group's strategies are the best way to handle a situation?

B. PICK A SITUATION:

Pick one situation from the list of temptations the boys came up with in the "Temptations Boys Face" exercise.

C. ROUND 1:

Let each team work separately on the temptation selected, deciding together what the right decision is, what reasons there are for making that decision, and how boys can best handle that kind of situation.

D. CASE PRESENTATION:

Each team should appoint a spokesperson for this round and then have each spokesperson present the team's case before the judges.

E. JUDGMENT:

The panel of judges should confer for no more than 10 minutes, rating each team from 1 to 4 on each of the three areas (decision, reasons, and strategies for handling). The team scoring the highest number of points wins the round. The trainer or a helper should assist the judges to make sure they discuss the relevant issues and to help them with the rating. With this system of rating, the judges don't have to agree. Each judge can give his own rating.

F. ROUND 2:

Repeat steps B, C, D, and E as many times as time permits.

PERSONAL APPLICATION

IDENTIFY:

Have each boy silently identify one temptation he is currently facing, one situation requiring integrity.

FATHERS/MENTORS:

If you think your boys will be comfortable, ask them to share with you all the steps below.

REASON:

Have your boys write out answers to the "Right and Wrong Checklist" for this situation.

DECISION:

Have each boy decide what the right thing to do is based on the checklist.

COMMIT:

Have the boys stand up, join hands, and silently commit to God and themselves their decision. FATHERS/MENTORS: Pray out loud with your boy if he has shared with you the temptation he is facing.

ASSIGNMENT FOR SESSIONS 15

Read *Forgive & Forget* (by Lewis Smedes available in paperback from Pocket Books).

CHOICES AUTHENTIC MEN KEEP MAKING

CHOICE 3 — CHOOSE TO WAIT SMART

This session teaches the boys the principle of delayed gratification. They learn to wait appropriately when the time for satisfaction of their needs and dreams has not yet come.

GOALS

At the end of this session, the boys will be able to:
1. Define the principle of delayed gratification.
2. Identify situations calling for delayed gratification.
3. Identify the three key components of smart waiting.
4. Commit to delaying gratification in certain key areas of their lives (including school distractions and sexuality) and identify strategies for doing so.

MATERIALS NEEDED

• This manual • Student workbooks • Bibles • The Oath of Manhood • The Road to Manhood map • Newsprint or chalkboard

WARM UP

1. Have your boys recite the Oath of Manhood. You may end in a prayer for learning and growth or a moment of quiet meditation on what they want to get out of this session. **FATHERS/MENTORS:** Recite the Oath with your boys.

VILLAGE TALK

2. Village Talk: This time is to provide boys with an opportunity to talk about the ways they have experienced various aspects of their manhood training since the last meeting.

OPENING ACTIVITY: AGREE/DISAGREE

WORKBOOK:
Have your boys turn in their workbooks to the "Agree/Disagree" exercise. Ask them to answer the questions quickly.

FATHERS/MENTORS:
Ask your boys to share their answers.

GROUP LEADERS:
Ask boys to raise their hands to see how many answered A and how many answered B.

ASK:
Ask each boy why he answered the way

he did. If he chose answer B (the delayed gratification choice), ask him "Are you really willing to go through all that effort?" Your intent is to get a sense of the boy's willingness to delay gratification.

GROUP LEADERS:

As each boy answers, put the results on the chalkboard or newsprint. After you have gotten their answers, point out the degree to which they are willing to wait for things to come.

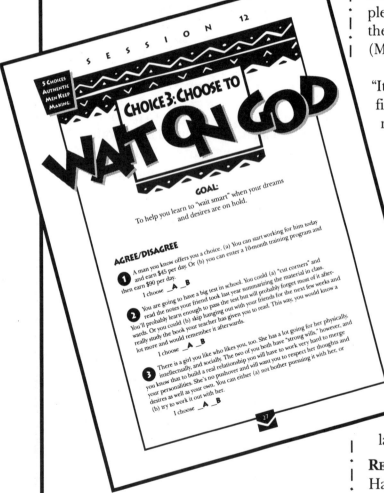

SESSION 12

5 CHOICES
AUTHENTIC
MEN KEEP
MAKING.

CHOICE 3: CHOOSE TO WAIT ON GOD

GOAL:

To help you learn to "wait smart" when your dreams and desires are on hold.

AGREE/DISAGREE

1 A man you know offers you a choice. (a) You can start working for him today and earn $45 per day. Or (b) you can enter a 10-month training program and then earn $90 per day.

I choose __A __B

2 You are going to have a big test in school. You could (a) "cut corners" and read the notes your friend took last year summarizing the material in class. You'll probably learn enough to pass the test but will probably forget most of it afterwards. Or you could (b) skip hanging out with your friends for the next few weeks and really study the book your teacher has given you to read. This way, you would know a lot more and would remember it afterwards.

I choose __A __B

3 There is a girl you like who likes you, too. She has a lot going for her physically, intellectually, and socially. The two of you both have "strong wills," however, and you know that to build a real relationship you will have to work very hard to merge your personalities. She's no pushover and will want you to respect her thoughts and desires as well as your own. You can either (a) not bother pursuing it with her, or (b) try to work it out with her.

I choose __A __B

27

SAY:

"Now we want to look at one of life's most important principles for you to learn. It's called the principle of delayed gratification. Everyone say it with me: 'DELAYED GRATIFICATION.'"

EXPLORATION

SAY:

"Let me tell you what delayed gratification means. Delaying gratification is a process of scheduling the pain and pleasure of life in a way that will enhance the pleasure by meeting and experiencing the pain first and getting it over with (M. Scott Peck, p. 19).

"It means to plan to do the hard things first so that you can then reap the rewards of your hard work. It means building a solid foundation before you try to put up a building. It means taking care of the essentials before you start on the non-essentials. It means doing your part before you worry about other people doing their part.

"Being willing to delay gratification means that you are willing to do whatever it takes to reach your goals in life.

"Now we are going to look at how Joseph's life demonstrates the importance of delayed gratification."

READ:

Have the boys take turns reading Genesis 39:20 through 40:23.

ASK:

1. "Where is Joseph right now, and why?"
> • *In prison because Potiphar's wife falsely accused him of trying to commit rape.*

2. "Does anyone have a relative in prison? (Wait for answers.) Do they enjoy it there? What is their daily life like there?

"Prisons today are boring and dangerous. Putting a group of men together who are inclined to break the law – perhaps even inclined to hurt or kill other people – and putting them in a situation where they don't have much freedom or interesting things to do, is a recipe for trouble. Prisons can be extremely difficult situations, sometimes deadly. Prison in Joseph's day was no better, perhaps even worse, although Joseph is in what was probably the best prison in the land, the prison where convicted officials of the Egyptian government were placed."

3. "What did we say is the first choice an authentic man makes?"
> • *Choose to excel, no matter what.*

4. "Do we see Joseph continuing to make this choice?"
> • *Yes, he doesn't give up; he does an excellent job and gets promoted.*

5. "As we look at chapter 40, what two major things does Joseph do while he is waiting in prison for his release?"
> • *Serves other people (through interpreting their dreams). Joseph, who was once so arrogant and insensitive to his brothers' feelings, has now become sensitive to other people's feelings (Genesis 40:6).*
> • *Makes the most of his opportunities .*
> a. *Uses his gifts of interpreting dreams.*
> b. *Makes a friend of the cupbearer and*

asks him to put in a good word for him.

SAY:

Have them turn in their workbooks to "Smart Waiting." Then say, "Joseph had to wait several years for his release. From his example, we can see that when you understand and accept the principle of delayed gratification, you are willing to wait for your dreams and wishes to come true. But while you are waiting, while your gratification is delayed, you learn to wait smart. Waiting smart involves three things which we learn from Joseph."

ASK:

"What are the three components of smart waiting?" Have them write the answers in their workbook while you write the answers on newsprint.

FATHERS/MENTORS:

Write them in your copy of the workbook.

> **P** = PATIENCE, which means "Trusting God to meet my needs and fulfill my dreams in His own time."

> **S** = SERVICE, which means "Meeting the needs of other people even when my own needs are on hold."

> **F** = FAITHFULNESS, which means "Making the most of every opportunity God gives me."

BREAK

(15 minutes for groups)

COMMITMENT: WAITING SMART WITH SEX

SAY:

"Now we will practice formulating a

strategy for smart waiting. Let's take the area of sexual gratification. We are going to come back to this until we have fully covered it. For now, let's accept the fact that God tells us to wait until marriage before we have sexual intercourse with a girl or a woman. Turn in your workbook to 'Waiting Smart with Sex.' How can you wait smart in this area and delay your gratification?"

SMART WAITING

To wait smart, you need . . .

1. **P** _____
Trusting God to meet my needs and fulfill my dreams in His own time.

2. **S** _____
Meeting the needs of other people even when my own needs are on hold.

3. **F** _____
Making the most of every opportunity God gives me.

WAITING SMART WITH SEX

To wait smart with sex, you need . . .

1. **P** _____
Trust God to choose a wife for me to enjoy in His own time.

2. **S** _____
Rather than using girls, I will learn to love them and meet their non-sexual needs.

3. **F** _____
I will learn to build a good relationship with girls step by step.

THE STEPS OF A GOOD RELATIONSHIP

1. _____
Meeting each other.

2. _____
Getting to know how each other thinks about everything.

3. _____
Beginning to share with each other your thoughts and feelings about God and being a Christian.

4. _____
Falling in love based on who I know the other person is.

5. _____
Expressing love through moderate physical expression (includes hugging and holding hands).

6. _____
Beginning to discuss merging our futures; we get engaged.

7. _____
Joining our lives totally with each other in marriage.

8. _____
Joining our bodies totally.

28

WRITE:
On newsprint, fill in the blanks as shown below. Have the boys fill in the blanks with you.

WAITING SMART WITH SEX

To wait smart with sex, you need . . .

1. **P** *(Patience)* Trust God to choose a <u>wife for me</u> to enjoy in His own time.

2. **S** *(Service)* Rather than using <u>girls, I will learn</u> to love them and meet their non-sexual needs.

3. **F** *(Faithfulness)* I will learn to <u>build a good relationship</u> with girls step-by-step.

DISCUSS:
Write on newsprint as you lead the boys in discussing the Steps of a Good Relationship.

Point out to the boys how every relationship with other people should start at Step 1 and progress as far as it can successfully. Most relationships will not go beyond Step 1. That should not be a problem for them. A number of relationships will go to Step 2. Fewer relationships will make it to Steps 3 and 4. Even fewer will make it to the higher steps. Stress the importance of the fact that one and only one relationship should progress to Steps 7 and 8.

THE STEPS OF A GOOD RELATIONSHIP

1. EYE-TO-EYE: Meeting each other.

2. MIND-TO-MIND: Getting to know how each other thinks about everything.

3. SPIRIT-TO-SPIRIT: Beginning to share with each other your thoughts and feelings about God and being a Christian.

4. HEART-TO-HEART: Falling in love based on who I know the other person is.

5. MOUTH-TO-MOUTH: Expressing love through moderate physical expression (includes hugging, holding hands).

6. FUTURE-TO-FUTURE: Beginning to discuss merging our futures; we get engaged.

7. LIFE-TO-LIFE: Joining our lives totally with each other in marriage.

8. PENIS-TO-VAGINA: Joining our bodies totally.

DISCUSS:

1. "What happens when we enter Stage 4 (we fall in love) before we have really done Stages 2 and 3?"

   • *TROUBLE. We fall in love and then we find out this girl we thought was wonderful is really terrible for us. Heartbreak time!!*

2. "What happens when we enter stage 5 before stages 2, 3 and 4?"

• *The relationship quickly becomes physical, and people never get to really know each other or discover true love. They lose out on the best parts of a relationship by focusing only on the physical aspects. Also, they never learn how to really get to know somebody, and then later they pick the wrong person to marry and end up divorced or in trouble.*

3. "What happens when we enter stage 8 before the other stages?"

   • *The same problems as just talked about, but ten times worse. We leave serious scars in girls' hearts. Real men don't use girls and break their hearts. We sometimes get venereal diseases like AIDS. We sin against God. And we lose our chance to build a great relationship.*

Point out that so many wives become disappointed in their husbands because the brothers only want sex and don't know how to romance a woman's mind and turn her on to him as a person on deep levels. The trainer can talk about other consequences as well.

PERSONAL REFLECTION
(5 minutes)

IDENTIFY:
Have each boy silently identify from the Steps of a Good Relationship which steps he knows about and is good at and which steps he is not. Point out that they may not have built a good relationship with girls; but they have built relationships with other boys, and many of the skills are the same.

COMMIT:
Have the boys stand, join hands, and silently commit to God and to each other

that they will learn to wait smart in the area of sexual gratification and learn now what they need to learn for a happy marriage.

ASSIGNMENT FOR SESSIONS 15

Read *Forgive & Forget* (by Lewis Smedes available in paperback from Pocket Books).

NOTES

_____

_____

_____

_____

_____

_____

_____

_____

_____

_____

_____

_____

_____

_____

_____

CHOICES AUTHENTIC MEN KEEP MAKING

CHOICE 4 — CHOOSE TO MOVE WHEN GOD'S TIME COMES

This session teaches the boys to learn to identify the signs of "God's time" and to move when God opens doors. This ability to move comes from good waiting.

GOALS

At the end of this session, the boys will be able to:
1. Identify the signs of God's moving on their behalf.
2. Identify in their life an open door they already have and commit to going for it.

MATERIALS NEEDED

• This manual • Student workbooks
• Bibles • The Oath of Manhood • The Road to Manhood map • Newsprint or chalkboard or pad of paper

WARM UP

1. Have your boys recite the Oath of Manhood. You may end in a prayer for learning and growth or a moment of quiet meditation on what they want to get out of this session. **FATHERS/MENTORS:** Recite the Oath with your boys.

VILLAGE TALK

2. Village Talk: This time is to provide boys with an opportunity to talk about the ways they have experienced various aspects of their manhood training since the last meeting.

OPENING ACTIVITY

ASK:
"Have you ever had an experience when you waited for something and then it finally came?"

DISCUSS:
Discuss with them the answers they come up with. Keep an eye out for similarities to the signs of God's moving that you will be teaching them in a few minutes. (For example, "It sounds like when we demonstrate that we can handle something, that's when doors start to open.")

SAY:
"Now we want to look at when doors were opened for Joseph so that we can learn when to look for doors to start opening

for us. There are no hard and fast rules that tell us when we're going to get breaks in life, but we know that if we wait smart, eventually the time will come for us to reap what we have sown."

EXPLORATION

READ:
Have the boys take turns reading Genesis chapters 40 and 41.

ASK:
1. "How does Joseph get out of prison?"
   • *Pharaoh has two dreams which no one can interpret. The cupbearer remembers that Joseph can interpret dreams. Joseph is summoned to interpret Pharaoh's dreams, which he does successfully.*
2. "Do you remember from last time what we said about how Joseph has grown as a person?" If hints are needed ask, "What kind of kid was Joseph like when he was young?"
   • *Arrogant, insensitive, self-centered.*
3. "What do we notice in Genesis 39:6 about Joseph's new sensitivity to people?"
   • *He took notice of the cupbearer's and baker's sadness.*
4. "What does that tell us about his growth and development?"
   • *That he has become more sensitive.*
5. "What did we notice last time about Joseph's willingness to serve other people?"
   • *That he was willing to serve them even when his own needs were on hold.*

SAY:
"So, we notice that Joseph has really grown in character during these difficult years while he has been in slavery and in

prison."

ASK:
1. "What does Joseph say Pharaoh's dreams mean?"
   • *That there are going to be seven great years, and then a severe famine is going to come for seven more years.*
2. "What does Joseph suggest Pharaoh do about it?"
   • *Prepare for it.*
3. "What does Pharaoh think of what Joseph has told him?"
   • *He feels extremely grateful and impressed and appoints Joseph to be in charge of getting Egypt ready for the famine.*
4. "What then, can we say is the reason for Joseph to be let out of prison at this point in time?"
   • *To help Egypt prepare for the famine.*

SAY:
"So, then, not only has Joseph grown in character, but there is a major task he has to accomplish that is critical for the nation of Egypt. In fact, not only is the famine to take place in Egypt, but also in the surrounding lands.

"And guess who is living in the surrounding lands? Joseph's father, brothers, and the rest of the family that has given him up for dead. They, too, will starve, unless Egypt is in a position to feed not only Egyptians but also everyone else around who wants to buy food.

"Fortunately, Joseph will be able to help not only the country of Egypt, but also his own people as well. He doesn't know it yet, but one day his starving family is

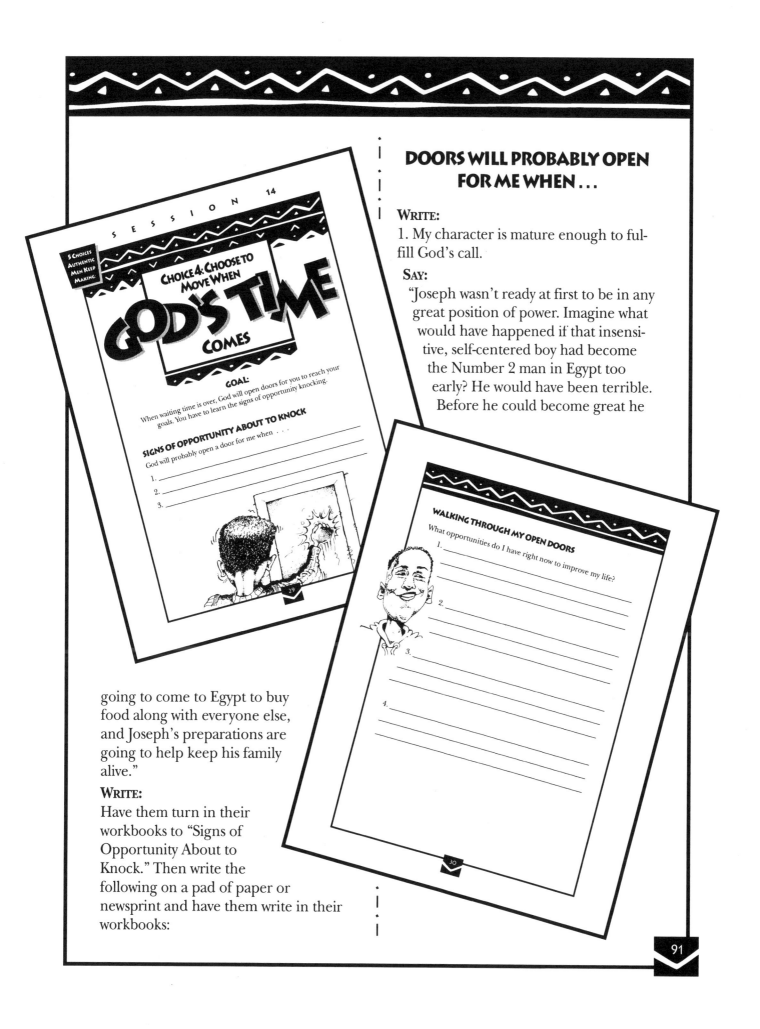

SESSION 14

5 CHOICES
AUTHENTIC
MEN KEEP
MAKING.

CHOICE 4: CHOOSE TO MOVE WHEN

GOD'S TIME

COMES

GOAL:

When waiting time is over, God will open doors for you to reach your goals. You have to learn the signs of opportunity knocking.

SIGNS OF OPPORTUNITY ABOUT TO KNOCK

God will probably open a door for me when . . .

1. _____
2. _____
3. _____

29

WALKING THROUGH MY OPEN DOORS

What opportunities do I have right now to improve my life?

1. _____
2. _____
3. _____
4. _____

30

DOORS WILL PROBABLY OPEN FOR ME WHEN . . .

WRITE:

1. My character is mature enough to fulfill God's call.

SAY:

"Joseph wasn't ready at first to be in any great position of power. Imagine what would have happened if that insensitive, self-centered boy had become the Number 2 man in Egypt too early? He would have been terrible. Before he could become great he going to come to Egypt to buy food along with everyone else, and Joseph's preparations are going to help keep his family alive."

WRITE:

Have them turn in their workbooks to "Signs of Opportunity About to Knock." Then write the following on a pad of paper or newsprint and have them write in their workbooks:

had to first learn sensitivity, service, and faithfulness as we discussed last time."

WRITE:

2. My opportunity is an opportunity to help other people.

SAY:

"Joseph's opportunity to get out of prison came when he was needed by many other people. Often we will find that when we are focused only on ourselves, our opportunities will be limited. But when we become men who are committed to helping other people, then we will have many opportunities that will help not only other people but also ourselves. Don't put the cart before the horse. Focus on serving others, and you may find yourself benefiting greatly."

WRITE:

3. God will get the glory.

SAY:

"While Joseph made the most of his limited opportunities by trying to get the cupbearer to remember him, the cupbearer forgot. It took God to give Pharaoh a dream for the cupbearer to remember his promise to Joseph two years before. That is what happens to us. We do our very best, but only God can make our 'best' successful. Our part is to do our best. His part is to open doors. And often he won't open doors until we are ready to acknowledge that He gets the credit. Doors will open in your life when you begin to really look to God to make your efforts successful.

"Of course, if you don't make any efforts, God is not likely to open any doors. But if you do your part, He will do his."

BREAK
(15 minutes for groups)

COMMITMENT: WALKING THROUGH MY OPEN DOORS

WORKBOOK:

Have them turn in their workbooks to "Walking Through My Open Doors." Have them fill out the exercise.

SAY:

"When God opens a door for you, you should go through it. Go for it. Never hold back. Do what God tells you to do, and He will give you the power to do it, because He has opened the door for you."

ASSIGNMENT FOR SESSIONS 15

Read *Forgive & Forget* (by Lewis Smedes available in paperback from Pocket Books).

CHOICES AUTHENTIC MEN KEEP MAKING

CHOICE 5 — CHOOSE TO LET GO OF THE PAST

This session shows boys how we can heal from and grow beyond the hurts of our past through forgiveness and authentic reconciliation.

GOALS

At the end of this session, boys will be able to:
1. Understand the natural process of forgiveness.
2. Identify a hurt they have experienced which they need to forgive.
3. Choose to let go of that hurt and begin to forgive the person.

MATERIALS NEEDED

• This manual • Student workbooks
• Bibles • The Oath of Manhood • The Road to Manhood map • *Forgive & Forget* (by Lewis Smedes available in paperback from Pocket Books).

ASSIGNMENT:
(In Sessions 12, 13, and 14, the boys were assigned to read *Forgive & Forget* for this session.)

WARM UP

1. Have your boys recite the Oath of Manhood. You may end in a prayer for learning and growth or a moment of quiet meditation on what they want to get out of this session. **FATHERS/MENTORS:** Recite the Oath with your boys.

VILLAGE TALK

2. Village Talk: This time is to provide boys with an opportunity to talk about the ways they have experienced various aspects of their manhood training since the last meeting.

OPENING ACTIVITY: FORGIVENESS – AGREE OR DISAGREE

WORKBOOK:
Have your boys turn in the workbook to "Forgiveness – Agree or Disagree." Let them answer the questions.

DISCUSS:
Talk with them about their answers. Don't tell them what you think.

PARABLE:
Read aloud to the boys the story of "The Magic Eyes" in Lewis Smedes' book, *Forgive & Forget.*

have to forgive. It usually does not come easily, but in time, it can come.

GROUP LEADERS:

Ask several men to share similar examples from their own pasts.

READ:

Have the boys take turns reading Genesis 42:1-25; 45:1-8.

EXPLAIN:

Explain to the boys the story in chapters 41 through 45. Explain how Joseph prepared Egypt for the famine. When the famine came, many people came to buy food from Egypt. Joseph's

---

SESSION 15

5 Choices Authentic Men Keep Making

CHOICE 5: CHOOSE TO LET GO OF THE PAST

GOAL:

To point out that every man is hurt on his journey to manhood. Being a hero means learning to forgive and let go of the hurtful past.

FORGIVENESS – AGREE OR DISAGREE

Circle "A" for Agree or "D" for Disagree:

1. **A D**   You can forgive someone, but you can never forget what they did.
2. **A D**   To forgive someone means you pretend they never hurt you.
3. **A D**   Forgiving one who hurts you is unfair. They should pay for what they did.
4. **A D**   If someone hurts me, I'm going to hurt them back.
5. **A D**   I should only forgive someone if they promise never to do it again.

HEALING MY HURTS

FORGIVENESS IS:

Being willing to make a new start with someone who hurt you when you didn't deserve it. (Lewis Smedes)

A process. When someone hurts you, you go through four stages:
• You hurt. • You feel anger.
• You heal. • You come back together and make a new start.

Person who hurt me is: _____

I felt hurt when: _____

The angry feelings I had were/are: _____

The new thoughts I have regarding myself are: _____

The new thoughts that have helped me survive and even move forward are: _____

The new choices regarding my relationships that have helped me survive and even move forward are: _____

The relationships that have helped me survive and even move forward are: _____

I AM READY TO FORGIVE AND MAKE A NEW START:

__ Yes   __ Not yet   __ Never

DISCUSS:

Talk with the boys about what they think the parable means, but try not to tell them what you think it means.

ELDER TALE:

Share with your boys an example of your having been hurt by someone and how you struggled to forgive that person. Help the boys understand that we all struggle when we

brothers came also, but Joseph made them go through a process of testing. He wanted to see if they felt guilty for what they had done to him. Genesis 42:21 shows they still were haunted by what they had done to Joseph. He also wanted to see if they would still sacrifice a brother (Benjamin) for their own welfare. It became clear to him that they had matured into men who were less selfish and who were now willing to go to jail for their brother's sake. Joseph then revealed who he was to them, forgave them, and made a new start with them. "God meant it for good," he said.

EXERCISE: HEALING THE HURTS I DID NOT DESERVE

DEFINE:
Have the boys turn in their workbooks to "Healing My Hurts." Read and discuss with them Smedes' definition of forgiveness – "making a new start." Then discuss the stages of forgiveness as Smedes talks about them. Point out how you went through some or all of those stages in the Elder Tale you told.

REFLECTION:
Have your boys think of a hurt they received that still makes them hurt or angry. Then help them go through the exercise. Ask them to talk about their answers, especially the last question. If they answered "Never" or "Not yet," ask them what it would take for them to heal enough to be ready to forgive the person.

As Smedes says, forgiveness is a process, not a choice. You can choose to get on with the process. You can't choose to heal. I don't push people to forgive. I push them to heal. Our boys are living in pain every day and reliving it and reliving it. They are not mature or independent enough not to be affected by it. What sustains them is the healing group created by their mentors. The group sustains them enough to go back into difficult situations. Leaders should stress that the boys go forward with their lives – make the best of their situation. Their attitude should be, "It may not be fair; it may be painful. But I'm going to make the best of my life." We acknowledge that it is not easy and see this attitude as a kind of an action forgiveness. Teach them not to do to others the same thing that others have done to them, but to go on.

FATHERS:
If you are the person they identify, be sure NOT to get defensive. Welcome the honest sharing of feelings. You are not a perfect father, so don't try to pretend that you are. This will be an excellent opportunity for both of you to grow.

HEALING PRAYER:
Lay hands on your boys and pray that God would heal them of the hurt. Pray for their will that they will choose to forgive, pray for their memories that God will ease the hurt and pain. Pray also for the relationship that may have been strained, that God would bring about true reconciliation (honest sharing of feelings, repentance, forgiveness).

THE POWER OF AN AUTHENTIC MAN

A RITE OF PASSAGE CELEBRATION

This session completes the boys' initial training in manhood. Its purpose is to summarize and to motivate them to live up to what they have learned.

GOALS

At the end of this session, boys will be able to:
1. Summarize what they have learned about manhood.
2. Affirm themselves as men-under-construction.

MATERIALS NEEDED

• This manual • A gift for each boy. The gift should be a symbol of what it means to be a man. Look around and see what is available. You want them to remember their Oath whenever they look at the gift.

WARM UP

1. Create an atmosphere of silence and mystery. Perhaps turn the lights down and light a candle, or do something else that will let the boys know this is not just another session. This is IT.

OPENING ACTIVITY: SUMMARIZE

REVIEW:
Ask your boys to review for you the meaning of each of the character traits in the Oath of Manhood. Ask them for an example of how they have seen that trait in their own life, even if it is only just beginning.

Then hold up the Road to Manhood Map and ask your boys to describe each of the steps and what the issues are at each step.

For both of these reviews, you may need to prompt their memories.

GROUP LEADERS:
Go around the room and make sure each boy gets to answer some of the traits and steps. Don't try to make each boy answer each one.

ELDER TALE:
Tell the boys what it has been like for you to teach them. What have you learned that has helped you become a better man?

RITE OF PASSAGE: RITUALIZE

READ:
Have a boy read I Corinthians 13:11.

SAY:
"It is time for you to begin putting childish ways behind you. I/we have tried to teach you something of what it means to be a man."

ASK:
Have each boy come stand before you and ask him, "Are you ready to start putting your childish ways behind you and become the man God wants you to become?"

PRAY:
When he answers "Yes," have him kneel before you (send boys who answer "no" back to their seats without comment. Talk to them privately afterwards). Lay your hands upon his head and pray for him. End your prayer by saying, "In the name of Jesus, I call you to be an authentic man of God. Amen. Stand up."

REWARD:
When the boy is standing, give him the gift you have selected, and say to him, "By receiving this gift, I/we can now expect you to start behaving like the man you have pledged to be. Say the Oath of Manhood."

GROUP LEADERS:
You may want to wait and have all the boys say the Oath together after they have each received their gift. It depends on your time.

CELEBRATE

It would be nice to have the parents of the boys at this session, or adult members of the church. Girls might also be invited. At the end, a party can be had for the boys, welcoming them onto the road to manhood.

RESOURCES TO HELP PREPARE BOYS FOR MANHOOD

SUGGESTED READINGS FOR WORKING WITH MALES

There are many resources on the market dealing with males. We have found the following to be excellent.

Adolescent Maltreatment: Issues and Program Models, "Issues of Adolescence." U.S. Department of Health and Human Services, Office of Human Development Services, Administration for Children, Youth, and Families.

Bly, Robert. *Iron John: A Book About Men.* Addison Wesley, 1990.

Campbell, Joseph. *The Hero with a Thousand Faces.*

Chariots of Fire (video).

Covey, Stephen, *The Seven Habits of Highly Effective People: Powerful Lessons in Personal Change.* New York: Simon & Schuster, 1989.

Dalbey, Gordon. *Healing the Masculine Soul.* Waco: Word, 1988.

Eisenman, Tom. *Temptations Men Face: Straightforward Talk on Power, Money, Affairs, Perfectionism, Insensitivity.* Downers Grove, Illinois: InterVarsity Press, 1990.

Frankl, Victor. *Man's Search for Meaning.*

Glory (video).

Hare, Nathan, and Julia Hare. *Bringing the Black Boy to Manhood: The Passage.* San Francisco: The Black Think Tank, 1985.

Hicks, Robert. *Uneasy Manhood: The Quest for Self-Understanding.* Nashville: Oliver-Nelson, 1991.

Kunjufu, Jawanza. *Countering the Conspiracy to Destroy Black Boys.* Chicago: African American Images, 1985.

Kunjufu, Jawanza. *Countering the Conspiracy to Destroy Black Boys, Vol. II.* Chicago: African American Images, 1986.

Moore, Robert and D. Gillette. *King, Warrior, Magician, Lover: Rediscovering the Archetypes of the Mature Masculine.* San Francisco: HarperCollins, 1990.

Osherson, Samuel. *Finding Our Fathers: How a Man's Life Is Shaped By His Relationship With His Father.* New York: Fawcett Columbine, 1986.

Osherson, Samuel. *Wrestling With Love: How Men Struggle With Intimacy With Women, Children, Parents, and Each Other.* New York: Fawcett Columbine, 1992.

Payne, Leanne. *Crisis in Masculinity.* Westchester, Illinois: Crossway Books, 1985.

Peck, M. Scott. *The Road Less Traveled: A New Psychology of Love, Traditional Values and Spiritual Growth.* New York: Simon Schuster, 1978.

Perkins, Useni. *Harvesting New Generations: The Positive Development of Black Youth.*

Project Manhood Operations Manual

Smedes, Lewis. *Forgive & Forget.* Pocket Books.

Tannen, Deborah. *You Just Don't Understand: Women and Men in Conversation.* New York: Balantine, 1990.

Wilson, Amos. *Black-On-Black Violence: The Psychodynamics of Black Self-Annihilation in Service of White Domination.* New York: Afrikan World Infosystems, 1990.

Wynn, Mychal. *Empowering African American Males to Succeed.*

SUGGESTIONS FOR CHURCH RITES OF PASSAGE ACTIVITIES

Should your church want to train boys to become men of God, the best option would be to contact us about implementing Project Manhood. This way, you don't have to reinvent the wheel, and can benefit from the experiences of other churches who have been working with African American boys. You may reach me at:

Project Manhood
Renaissance Productions
537 Mantua Avenue – Suite 203
Woodbury, NJ 08096

However, the following are some suggested Rites of Passage activities which your church can use to assist you as you take your boys through the *Let the Journey Begin* manual:

RITES OF PASSAGE ACTIVITIES

1. Designate a special uniform and place for the boys to sit in church services once a month.

2. Have the boys come before the church periodically to recite their Oath of Manhood (individually or together).

3. Have the boys come before the church and have the men of the church surround the boys, lay hands on them and pray for them.

4. Read to the congregation the report cards of boys who have made improvements in their grades or attendance.

5. Give the boys in the training group some "masculine" tasks in the church as a group (e.g., junior security guards, a clean up campaign). Be sure to make the tasks seem important, and not just free labor.

6. For boys who complete each module of the manuals, give them some kind of public reward or award, and spell out to the congregation the growth that has been seen in them.

TIPS FOR LEADING GROUP DISCUSSIONS

1. LISTEN FAR MORE THAN YOU SPEAK.
You will probably have a lot you want to say to the boys, but hold back so that they will feel more comfortable sharing. Try not to interject comments that stop the boys from talking, such as:

- *"You'll be fine."*
- *"It's not so bad. Stop pitying yourself."*
- *"You're not really feeling . . . (angry, sad, hopeless, etc.)."*

Remember, feelings are not wrong, they just are. It's what we do with our feelings that counts.

Watch your body language. Look at a boy who is talking. Perhaps go put your arm around him if he is evidencing a struggle.

2. ASK GOOD QUESTIONS.
Many of the questions you need to ask the boys are spelled out in the manual. But no manual can cover everything, so you will need to ask follow-up questions and questions that will help boys explore the topic more fully. Good questions:

- *Should be clear and specific, not vague.*
- *Should not be too long or complex. If they are too long, break them down into separate questions.*
- *Should generate discussion. Avoid questions that can be answered in one word (e.g. "yes" or "no").*
- *Should encourage the boys to think for themselves.*

3. DON'T ANSWER YOUR OWN QUESTIONS.
If the question is not understood, repeat it or rephrase it. When people think that you will do most of the talking, they will become quiet and passive.

4. DON'T BE AFRAID OF SILENCE.
Sometimes boys need some time to think. Try to distinguish, however, between the times when people are thinking and when the question is unclear or irrelevant.

5. DON'T BE CONTENT WITH JUST ONE ANSWER.
Other contributions will add depth and richness to the discussion. Ask the others what they think or ask if anyone has other ideas until several people have had a chance to speak.

6. BE AFFIRMING.

Boys will be more willing to contribute if they feel their answers are genuinely appreciated – even if you disagree. Thank boys for their contributions. Praise boys when they have answered a difficult question or made a good point. You can also say things like, "That's a good point," "I really never thought of it in that way before," or "That is very helpful. It shows us that . . . "

7. SUMMARIZE PERIODICALLY.

Don't let the discussion drag. Summarize the points so far, point to the Road to Manhood Map or other materials to help boys see constantly where they are, etc. Keep things moving.

8. STICK TO THE TOPIC UNDER DISCUSSION.

Resist the temptation to go after interesting but unnecessary ideas. If there are additional topics you want the boys to look at, schedule additional sessions. We, in fact, encourage that. The manual is really meant to give you some help in training boys, not to do all of it for you.

9. MAINTAIN CONFIDENTIALITY.

What is shared in the group stays in the group. You will have to use great wisdom in sharing anything with boys' parents. Be very, very careful. Make sure it is absolutely necessary to do so.

Some Common Problems and How to Handle Them

1. Boys Who Monopolize the Discussion.

• Examine yourself. Are you monopolizing the discussion?

• Direct questions to specific boys. That way, the monopolizers can't answer it, or if they do, you can stop them.

• Say, "Let's hear from those who haven't said anything yet."

• Avoid looking at the talkers, or responding to their comments.

• Speak to them privately after the meeting.

2. Answers That Are Obviously Wrong.

• Don't shame the boy who made the comment. Still thank him for his contribution.

• Don't contradict the boy yourself, but ask other group members what they think or ask them if they have a different opinion. Then when they give the right answer, affirm it as the right answer.

• Ask the boy what led him to that conclusions.

3. Disruptive Behavior.

• Follow your group rules consistently.

• Any violations of the rules should be dealt with immediately. Younger boys, especially, need immediate feedback.

• Develop a system of rewards for good behavior as well as punishments for bad behavior. That way, boys won't act up just to get attention. They can get attention by acting properly.

• Be prepared for what Dr. Jawanza Kunjufu calls "The Showdown," in which your authority and courage are tested by the boys. Don't lose the showdown. You must remain in charge, but remain calm and loving as you assert your control over the group.

SUGGESTED JOB DESCRIPTIONS

For a project to function smoothly, everyone needs to know his duties, his responsibilities, and the extent of his authority. These will be summarized below. It should be noted that education and training are important and may be obtained formally or informally on the job. While we do not specify what educational attainment is prerequisite for the various positions, we encourage careful gift discernment in staffing decisions. In addition, the wise pastor and/or project director will surround the project with advisors and consultants who have demonstrated expertise in the social sciences and administration.

An adequate training program should be conducted prior to launching your Project Manhood. Consistent ongoing training and staff meetings will help ensure that your staff will have a growing set of skills for assisting boys on their journey to manhood.

Depending on the availability of personnel, one person may hold two or more of the following positions:

PROJECT DIRECTOR JOB DESCRIPTION

FUNCTION:
Serves as the overall leader, developer, and spokesperson for the local Project Manhood.

QUALIFICATIONS:
• Administrative skills, particularly in program design, planning, and implementation; supervisory skills; and staff training experience.

• Public speaking ability: Must be able to represent Project Manhood to the larger community.

• Marketing/Public Relations Skills: Should be able to develop and implement strategies for raising public awareness of the program and raising funds to support it.

• The project director should be a male in order to model male leadership to the boys.

DUTIES:
• Develop a comprehensive plan for implementing Project Manhood in his locale.

• Select appropriate sites for project implementation and negotiate all arrangements.

• Help recruit and select the key personnel for the project. Provide detailed orientation and training to them directly and/or through training programs and seminars available locally and nationally.

• Develop an operating budget and, as necessary, raise funds to support the project.

• Identify and negotiate working agreements (linkages and partnerships) with community resources that will be necessary for the project.

• Select curriculum materials to use with the boys and their parents. Train staff in their use.

• Develop specific policies and procedures for the project consistent with project guidelines contained in the Project Manhood Operations Manual.

• Oversee recruitment and selection of project participants.

• Supervise project staff, ensuring implementation of Project Manhood in accordance with the Project Manhood comprehensive plans and policies developed for the program.

• Oversee the evaluation of the project.

• Communicate the goals, objectives, plans, needs, and successes of Project Manhood to the larger community in writing and orally.

• Motivate, discipline, and terminate paid and volunteer project staff. As

appropriate, participate in decisions regarding project participants.

• Perform whatever other duties are required to ensure successful project implementation.

PROJECT COORDINATOR JOB DESCRIPTION

FUNCTION:
Serves as the day-to-day administrator of the local Project Manhood, ensuring smooth and effective implementation of all aspects of the project.

REPORTING RELATIONSHIP:
Reports to Project Director.

QUALIFICATIONS:
• Three years' experience in operating a significant program (not necessarily an organization, but at least a major program or project within an organization) and supervising staff.

• Gender: Male.

DUTIES:
• Give day-to-day supervision and oversight to Project Manhood.

• Participate in recruiting and selecting project staff who will report to him.

• Provide ongoing supervision to project staff.

• Schedule all project activities; arrange logistics; and ensure smooth implementation of all activities.

• Conduct training sessions for project participants.

• Gather all necessary data on project participants for case management and evaluation functions.

• Ensure that all policies, procedures, and plans developed by Project Director are carried out.

• Communicate regularly with community agencies and other resources to ensure smooth linkages.

• Recruit mentors and other volunteer staff.

• Search out community opportunities for project participants to take advantage of.

• Perform other duties as assigned.

PARENT TRAINER JOB DESCRIPTION

FUNCTION:
Serves as the lead trainer of parents in the local Project Manhood.

REPORTING RELATIONSHIP:
Reports to Project Coordinator.

QUALIFICATIONS:
• Four years' training experience, including two years of training adults in social service settings using written curricula.

• Good understanding of parenting issues and issues related to raising African American boys.

DUTIES:
• Provide training workshops to parents of the boys in the program using curricula selected by the Project Director.

• Form a basic assessment of each family in the program and communicate assessment in writing to Project Coordinator.

• Train selected parents in leading parent support groups and assist such groups to form.

• Advise and train project staff about family issues and how best to help the boys, given their family issues.

CASE MANAGER JOB DESCRIPTION

FUNCTION:
Serves as a paid or volunteer assistant to the Project Director and/or the Project Coordinator.

REPORTING RELATIONSHIP:
Reports to Project Director or Project Coordinator, depending on whom he is assisting.

QUALIFICATIONS:
• Prior experience requirement varies depending on duties assigned.

• Personal: Has personal maturity and has life in order (for example, not newly in recovery from addiction, a reasonable work history, a reasonably stable personality, no history of child abuse).

• Gender: Front-line assistants (those who work with boys) should be male.

"Back office" assistants may be either male or female.

DUTIES:

• Provide case management to a caseload of boys in the program, ensuring that they get all the counseling and other services from community resources that they need.

• Assist with boys' training sessions.

• Assist with logistics of project activities.

• Provide mentoring to the boys.

PREREQUISITES FOR A SUCCESSFUL PROJECT MANHOOD

You can see from this manual that Project Manhood is a well-planned, ambitious project which requires a good deal of commitment. But ask yourself if boys aren't worth everything you can give. As you plan to embark on a journey to train boys to become men, review the following checklist with the other members of your planning team.

MOTIVATION

• Why do you want to do Project Manhood? It can be a difficult, demanding program or ministry. It requires a substantial commitment of time, energy, and creativity. You need volunteers who will go the distance. Are you truly committed to reaching a generation of boys to help them become authentic men?

MISSION AND PHILOSOPHY

• Is your group/organization substantially committed to the goals and objectives of Project Manhood? Do you want to foster the values, attitudes, skills, and habits that Project Manhood promotes.

WHO SHOULD OPERATE A PROJECT MANHOOD?

• Project Manhood requires a long-term commitment to boys, ideally a generation of boys. Therefore, Project Manhood should be operated by a group which would have consistency and stability. Does your group have this consistency and stability?

• To be successful, Project Manhood requires a group of men. Will your group/organization be able to provide – or does it have the potential to soon provide – sufficient numbers of men to fill the job descriptions in the Operations Manual? While you may not have enough men so that each boy can have a mentor, will you have enough men so that Case Managers have no more than eight boys each?

• Project Manhood's design serves groups of boys better than an individual boy. Can your group/organization reach an entire peer group; that is, a social network of boys?

RESOURCES

• PLACE: Where will your meetings with boys take place? Is the space adequate? Will you get it consistently?

• FINANCES: While Project Manhood can operate with volunteers, our experience indicates that the core staff should receive some remuneration for their services. They work very hard, and they are the glue that holds volunteers together. In addition, Project Manhood requires other kinds of expenditures such as food, T-shirts, jackets, transportation, retreats, sports equipment, curricula, etc. You should carefully review the program components, decide which ones you will implement first, and make out a budget. Do you have sufficient resources?

• STAFF: Do you have men with the qualifications needed to fill the job descriptions suggested for Project Manhood? Do you have people who can train your staff to implement the program (or will you commit to engaging the national team of Project Manhood to train your staff)?

COMMUNITY LINKAGES

• Does your group/organization have – or can it develop – good contacts with the kinds of community agencies and ministries which Project Manhood requires?